Lonnie E. Dver
L. C. C.
1966

WORLD CONQUEST

WORLD CONQUEST

by

PAUL B. SMITH, B.A., D.D., F.R.G.S.

Pastor of The Peoples Church, Toronto

Foreword by

REV. G. CHRISTIAN WEISS, D.D.

*Missionary Director, Back to the Bible
Broadcast, Lincoln, Nebraska*

London
MARSHALL, MORGAN & SCOTT
Edinburgh

LONDON
MARSHALL, MORGAN AND SCOTT, LTD.
1–5 PORTPOOL LANE
HOLBORN, E.C.1

AUSTRALIA
117–119 BURWOOD ROAD
MELBOURNE, E.13

SOUTH AFRICA
P.O. BOX 1720, STURK'S BUILDINGS
CAPE TOWN

CANADA
EVANGELICAL PUBLISHERS
241 YONGE STREET
TORONTO

THE PEOPLES PRESS
100 BLOOR STREET EAST
TORONTO

U.S.A.
WORLD LITERATURE CRUSADE PRESS
BOX 1314, STUDIO CITY
CALIFORNIA

MADE AND PRINTED IN GREAT BRITAIN BY PURNELL AND SONS, LTD.
PAULTON (SOMERSET) AND LONDON

To My Father
OSWALD J. SMITH, Litt.D.
from whom I have learned much
of what I may know about Missions

FOREWORD

Between the time the author of this book requested that I write a brief Foreword and the time of this actual writing, God reached into my home and family without warning and took away the richest treasure I had in the whole wide world, my wife, Olga. Now more than ever before I feel there is but one chief purpose for which to live: the evangelization of the world.

She and I sat together at a Bible conference in western Nebraska and listened to Paul Smith deliver numbers of these present messages from an overflowing heart. We thanked God for his impassioned presentation and plea then, and I thank Him now for moving upon the Preacher's heart to make these messages available to the Church at large.

The Church in this generation *could* evangelize the world. I say this with deliberation. With the revolutionary avenues at our disposal today, no one can successfully gainsay this. Transportation has increased by one thousand times and communication by ten thousand during my lifetime. Apart from spiritual power, which is most assuredly available to us, what more is needed to proclaim Christ to the entire race than vehicles of transportation and communication? If we fail to carry out this God-ordained and Bible-revealed Mission we will surely stand indicted before the judgment seat of Christ in the day when we shall be judged for the deeds done in the body.

It has been my conviction for several years that unless pastors, leaders and instructors in our Christian training institutions get a vision for Missions, such a vision is hardly possible to the Church as a whole. I thank God that the two men, father and son, who have pastored the renowned Peoples Church of Toronto have had this vision. And I am grateful that this added potent contribution is now being put in print by Dr. Paul Smith, my friend and fellow-servant of Jesus

Christ and of the world. I appeal especially to pastors and religious leaders to study the messages contained in this volume and to *pass them on* to the people under their spiritual direction and care.

G. Christian Weiss, D.D., F.R.G.S.

PREFACE

For more than a quarter of a century there has been a Missionary Convention every year in The Peoples Church. One entire month is set aside for this, the most important event in our church calendar. There have been two sessions every day of the week, afternoon and evening, with two speakers at each session. I have been at the convention every year for more than twenty-five years. It has been my privilege to sit under the ministry of most of the great missionary statesmen of this generation, and to associate with hundreds of missionaries from all over the globe. Some of the greatest are now with the Lord.

The great principles I have tried to set forth in this book have been learned over a period of many years of saturation in a missionary atmosphere. These are not ideals that cannot be realized. The Peoples Church stands as a monument to the fact that they work. I have seen the same principles introduced in many other churches, and they have been revolutionized as a result.

Much of what I know about world evangelization I have learned from my father, and I am quite aware of the fact that when it comes to missions, although I may have the advantage of stepping from the shoulders of a great father, the only direction I can step is down. I pray that God will give me the grace to walk on the lower level.

P. B. S.

Toronto, Canada
December, 1959

CONTENTS

PART I

THE MOTTOES THAT MOTIVATE THE MEMBERS

PART II

THE MONEY THAT MOVES THE MACHINERY

PART III

The Marks that Make the Missionary

PART I

THE MOTTOES THAT MOTIVATE THE MEMBERS

"How shall they hear without a preacher?"

CHAPTER I

NOT MAYBE BUT MUST

FROM THE BIBLE

"Afterward he appeared unto the eleven as they sat at meat, and upbraided them with their unbelief and hardness of heart, because they believed not them which had seen him after he was risen. And he said unto them, Go ye into all the world, and preach the gospel to every creature. He that believeth and is baptized shall be saved; but he that believeth not shall be damned" (Mark 16: 14–16).

CHAPTER I

NOT MAYBE BUT MUST

THE Great Commission is not one of the *maybe's* of the Bible but a *must*.

When I was courting my wife her mother used to serve us tea out of the most enormous green tea-pot I have ever seen. Her family was large, and they were all within a limited age bracket. This meant that every time we sat down to a meal we looked somewhat like the young people's society of a church having a tea meeting. The girls in the family would invite their boy friends, and the boys their girl friends.

The amazing thing about the green tea-pot was that it never seemed to run dry. It could supply tea for as many as were present regardless of the number. At the beginning of the meal the tea would be so powerful that it would almost support the weight of a spoon. Toward the mid-point it had become only half as strong, and by the last round it would be extremely weak. Obviously what had happened, was that the potency had been gradually reduced by the addition of more boiling water. It was a *must* at the first; it was a *maybe* at the last. No one questioned the fact that it was tea in the beginning, but there was a great deal of doubt toward the end.

In the Bible there are some verses that for certain people have become *maybe's*. As a result of higher criticism, some men have had to put a circle around passages of Scripture and write *maybe* across them. Others have written *maybe* as far as the meaning is concerned. Still others look upon some parts with a *maybe* in regard to application.

Higher Criticism

Everybody knows that the higher critics have almost completely discarded a great deal of the Bible because they feel that in places it is not authentic, not accurate, or not in agreement with the rest of the Bible. The passage from which we normally take the Great Commission is a case in point. Because the last eight verses of Mark have not appeared in the oldest manuscripts, the higher critics doubt their authenticity. For many years the Epistle of James was held in great doubt. Some thought it had no place among the other inspired writings. Thus the higher critics have gone through their Bible writing the word *maybe* across a number of the verses and chapters.

When we are faced with the Great Commission, however, we find ourselves confronted with a command that has never been weakened despite all the attacks of the higher critics. If it is taken from Mark 16, it appears again in Mark 13: 10, "And the gospel must first be published among all nations." Remove it from the Gospel of Mark and we find it again in Luke 24: 47, "And that repentance and remission of sins should be preached in His name among all nations." If you doubt the Gospels, you can find it in the Acts of the Apostles, "But ye shall receive power, after that the Holy Ghost is come upon you: and ye shall be witnesses unto me both in Jerusalem, and in all Judea, and in Samaria, and unto the uttermost part of the earth" (Acts 1: 8). Even if it is erased entirely from the New Testament, it can be seen in prophetic form all through the Old Testament. "Declare His glory among the heathen, His wonders among all people" (Psalm 96: 3).

"Go ye into all the world, and preach the gospel to every creature" still stands as the Great Commission even for the higher critics. It is not one of the *maybe's* of the Bible, but a *must*.

Meaning

The very fact that there are a number of different denominations indicates that there is a wide variety of views among Christian people, as far as the meaning of Scripture is concerned. In some cases there may be as many as a score of different interpretations of the same verses or chapters.

No one could possibly deny the fact that the word *baptism* to some Christians means immersion, to others it means sprinkling, and to still others it means pouring. Men have written *maybe* around baptism as far as meaning is concerned.

Eternal security is another issue about which there has been great difference of opinion. One half of the Church believes that when a man is saved he can never be lost again. The other half has always believed that it is possible to fall from grace and be lost even after there has been a sound conversion. Theologians call the first group Calvinists, and the other group Arminians. Obviously, the Church has written *maybe* across the verses in the Bible that deal with the security or lack of security of the believer as far as their meaning is concerned.

The greatest diversity of interpretation is seen in the prophetic Scriptures. Read the various expositions by evangelical men on such books as Ezekiel, Daniel, and Revelation. Although we all believe the great essentials and agree about them, there is no doubt that on other prophetic points there is as much difference of opinion as there is difference in the names of the men who write. All through the prophetic books the expositors have written *maybe* when it comes to interpretation.

Let me digress from the main course of my theme to say this: After a great deal of travel and contact with Christian brethren around the world, I have become thoroughly convinced that although we often differ from the doctrinal standpoint on some issues, spiritual Christians agree perfectly in the practical outcome of their lives. The spiritual Calvinist and the spiritual Arminian live the same kind of lives. Their differences are in their language, not their lives. The carnal Christian differs from the spiritual Christian in both language and life.

The Calvinist who is spiritual is so grateful to God for his eternal security that he does everything within his power to live a life pleasing to God. The Arminian who is spiritual does not want to fall from grace, and so he, too, lives for God to the best of his ability. Thus the two men discover that although they call the street by a different name and were brought by different vehicles, they are walking down the same road together.

Carnal men do just the opposite. The Calvinist uses his eternal security as a licence to live as he pleases, whereas the Arminian becomes discouraged because he may lose his salvation and throws up his hands in despair, making no attempt to live for God. Thus both men walk along the street of carnality, but they do not walk together. One is on this side of the street and the other is on that side, because they do not speak the same language.

The Apostle Paul called the Corinthians carnal because of their divisions. "For ye are yet carnal: for there is among you envying, and strife, and divisions, are ye not carnal, and walk as men?" (1 Cor. 3: 3).

However, when it comes to the meaning of the Great Commission, there can be no difference of interpretation. There is no *maybe* about the meaning. The words are simple and direct: "Go . . . world . . . preach . . . gospel . . . every creature." Whatever your denominational affiliation may be, the Commission remains the same. Other differences there may be, but there is no difference here. The interpretation could be made by a child. Take the Gospel to everybody in the world.

Application

If anywhere in the Bible there is a picture of the nucleus of the Christian Church, this is it. Mark makes it clear that Jesus is not talking to a group of the general public, as He had done on many other occasions. Nor is He addressing the Jewish nation. He is talking directly to "the eleven". Judas had killed himself, and Jesus was taking this opportunity after His resurrection to commission the other disciples.

These were the men whom He had picked personally to follow Him. These were the men that had been with Him throughout His earthly ministry. These were the men who were to be in the upper room on the day of Pentecost, and these were the men who were to preach the first Gospel messages. This was the nucleus of the Church of God—the living body of Christ; and it was to this group that Jesus issued the command.

Thus there can be no *maybe* as to its application. If you are a member of the family of God, if you form a part of the living body of Christ, if you belong to the Church, the command applies to you. Sometimes people ask if they should be missionary-minded. If you are not missionary-minded, you are not living in the will of God. Often the pastor wonders if his church would do better if there were a missionary emphasis. No church has any reason for its existence if it is not a missionary church, with a world-wide emphasis.

The power of the Holy Ghost promised in the first chapter of Acts is not given that the Christian may enjoy an unusual religious experience. It is given that the Christian may take the Gospel to the world. "But ye shall receive power, after that the Holy Ghost is come upon you: and ye shall be witnesses unto me both in Jerusalem, and in all Judea, and in Samaria, and unto the uttermost part of the earth" (Acts 1: 8).

The command was issued to the Church, and if you are in the Church it is your duty to obey it. There may be doubt in the minds of some as to the application of certain passages of Scripture, but there can be no *maybe* when it comes to the application of the Great Commission.

Give the Gospel to the world. This is a spiritual imperative. In its authenticity, its meaning, and its application. The Great Commission is not one of the *maybe's* of the Bible, but a *must*.

CHAPTER II

NOT DONE BUT DO

FROM THE BIBLE

"When they therefore were come together, they asked of him, saying, Lord, wilt thou at this time restore again the kingdom to Israel? And he said unto them, It is not for you to know the times or the seasons, which the Father hath put in his own power. But ye shall receive power, after that the Holy Ghost is come upon you: and ye shall be witnesses unto me both in Jerusalem, and in all Judea, and in Samaria, and unto the uttermost part of the earth. And when he had spoken these things, while they beheld, he was taken up; and a cloud received him out of their sight" (Acts 1: 6-9).

CHAPTER II

NOT DONE BUT DO

THE verb of the Great Commission is not *done* but *do*. After nearly two thousand years of Church history the tense of the Christian's task is not past but future. We have not done the job; it remains to be done. From the standpoint of place, population, and publication, the task is far from complete.

Place

There are great areas of the world's surface that have not yet felt the pressure of a missionary's footsteps. There are huge spaces of the air that man breathes that have never carried the sound waves of a missionary's voice. There are people living in these areas breathing the air but with no opportunity to hear the message of God's salvation. They form a part of the "world" for which God gave His Son.

To the north of my own country, the Dominion of Canada, there are vast stretches of snowbound land where men and women live who have never seen a missionary. They are a scattered, isolated people, difficult to reach, but a part of the world. There are no market places where hundreds can be found at one time. There are no towns where meetings can be held. There is a family here, a family there; a tiny community alone in the wilderness of snow and ice—Eskimo, Indian and Russian, just able to keep body and soul together in a hard land.

Tibet and Afghanistan are similar, with very few places that could be called towns but supporting scattered groups of people who live in almost total isolation from civilization, sometimes in the midst of snow and ice, other times in the heart of rugged mountain ranges, and often in both. These and other areas like them constitute the greatest challenge

25

possible. There is no glory or glamour or glitter about ministering there. They are hard places to get into, and harder to live in after an entry has been made. There are no crowds and few converts. It is a ministry from tent to tent, igloo to igloo, shack to shack, with hundreds of miles of tortuous trail between.

Geographically, the task has not been completed. Many are the places where men have lived for centuries that have yet to see their first missionary. These form a part of the world for which Christ died.

Population

Not only have we failed to go to all the places geographically, but we have failed to reach the people of the more densely-populated areas with the Gospel.

There are probably two billion, eight hundred million people in the world to-day. Over half of them have never been evangelized despite the fact that the Church has had her orders for nearly twenty centuries. Where are they? There are 70 million in Africa, 75 million in South America, 35 million in the islands of the sea, 50 million in Japan, 250 million in China, 250 million in India, 40 million in South East Asia, 34 million in Central Asia, and 250 million in Europe.

All of these are conservative figures. In some countries an exact census is difficult to take. In India and particularly China the populations are probably larger than estimated, which would make the number of unevangelized people greater. From the standpoint of population the task is far from completion.

Publication

Undoubtedly, the area in which we have failed miserably is the publication of the Word of God. We used to think there were approximately two thousand spoken languages in the world. A recent survey by organizations who make it their business to know, has revealed that there are at least three thousand languages in use to-day.

The Wycliffe Bible Translators tell us that of these languages only 206 have the entire Bible, 260 have the New Testament, 618 have less than the New Testament, and 100 have less than one book. This means that there are at least two thousand individual languages used by people who have yet to see the first verse of the Word of God in their own language.

Where are some of these languages that we did not know existed before? In New Guinea there are 626. There are 200 among the Aboriginals of Australia. Another 200 among the islands of Indonesia, and 321 are to be found on other Pacific islands. These places represent a total of 1,300 languages, and of these only 100 have some part of the Bible, leaving 1,200 in these areas alone with no portion of Scripture whatsoever.

In some of these places the people speak their own language and also the language of some foreign nation that has ruled them. For instance, most of the North American Indians speak their tribal Indian language, but they can also speak, and in many cases read and write, the English language. Missionaries are working hard to reduce the Indian languages to writing, and then to translate the Bible into them. The question arises, why waste the time doing this when you could give them an English Bible that has already been printed?

The answer is simple to the missionary or to anyone who knows anything about linguistics. There is a language of the lips, a language of the head, and a language of the heart. When you go to a foreign country you can quickly memorize enough words and phrases so that you can find your way about. A person who has done this has not really learned the language. He thinks of everything in his native tongue first, and then translates it into the foreign phrases he has memorized. It is only when you have begun to think in the foreign language that you can really say you know it. People who have lived for some years in a foreign land usually learn to do this. Their minds have been trained to use a new linguistic vehicle.

However, no matter how fluently a man may learn to speak

and think in a foreign language, it never becomes the language of his heart. The important transactions of his personal life must be done in his native tongue. We have a great many immigrants in Canada from Continental Europe. Some of them have been there for years. They have learned English well. They speak it, write it, and do their business in it; but when it comes to their spiritual life the transactions must be made in the language of their hearts. There are scores of European folk in Canada that still pray and read their Bibles in the language of their homeland although they have been in Canada for years.

It is very difficult to reach the North American Indian with the Gospel in the English language. He understands it, but it remains the language of his head, and when the message is given to him in English he thinks of it as the white man's religion. When he hears the Gospel in the language his mother and father used during his boyhood it speaks to his heart. Any Gospel that merely reaches a man's head is of little value, but the message that gets through to his heart will revolutionize him.

That is why it is essential that we bend every effort to get the Word of God into the language of the people—not just a language they can speak, but a language that can speak to them. This gigantic part of the task of world evangelism has not been done.

Before you become a Christian the tense of the Bible is past. There is nothing to do, only believe. "It is finished." The moment you accept Christ as your Saviour, the tense changes. Then comes the command, "Be ye doers of the word, and not hearers only" (James 1: 22). When Jesus gave the disciples the Great Commission the verb was not *done* but *do,* and sad to say after two thousand years of Church history the verb is still not *done* but *do.*

CHAPTER III

NOT SYSTEMS BUT SATAN

FROM THE BIBLE

"Finally, my brethren, be strong in the Lord, and in the power of his might. Put on the whole armour of God, that ye may be able to stand against the wiles of the devil. For we wrestle not against flesh and blood, but against principalities, against powers, against the rulers of the darkness of this world, against spiritual wickedness in high places. Wherefore take unto you the whole armour of God, that ye may be able to withstand in the evil day, and having done all, to stand" (Eph. 6: 10–13).

CHAPTER III

NOT SYSTEMS BUT SATAN

THE struggle of the missionary is not against *systems* but *Satan*.

This principle applies not only to the work of the missionary, but also to the work of the Christian at home. It is not our business to fight the systems of this world. Our task is to wage war against Satan, who is the power behind the systems. "For we wrestle not against flesh and blood, but against principalities, against powers, against the rulers of the darkness of this world, against spiritual wickedness in high places" (Eph. 6: 12).

When we pray we are not seeking the destruction of systems; we are praying for the overthrow of Satan. When we give, we are not giving that systems may be abolished; we are giving that Satan may be defeated. When we witness by life or word, our target is not to tear down systems; we are witnessing that Satan may be thwarted. When the missionary goes to the foreign field, he does not go to wrestle against flesh and blood; he goes to combat the hosts of Satan that are the real foe of the work of God.

Not long ago I was driving north on one of our Canadian highways with a friend. It was late at night, but there was a steady stream of holiday traffic going both ways. The car immediately in front of us was being driven quite normally, but ahead of this car there was a small delivery truck careening crazily back and forth across the road, obviously driven by some quite inebriated individual. Cars coming from the opposite direction were in great danger of meeting the truck in a head-on collision. One after another passed perilously close, some of them being forced right off the highway to avoid an accident.

The driver of our car was determined somehow to get this truck, which was a menace to everybody, off the road. It had to be stopped. Human life was in danger. It was a simple matter to pass the car in front of us, but it took much longer to find a good opportunity to pass the truck which was still moving in serpentine fashion along the highway. At last we managed to get by, and with a gradual application of the brakes we were able to force the truck to a standstill.

It was one thing to stop the truck temporarily, but quite another to stop it permanently. How were we to do it? Should we go back to the truck and begin to pound the mudguards with our fists, kick at the tyres, break the glass in the windows, and scratch at the paint on the doors? Of course not. Our job was to remove the driver from the driver's seat, and the truck would be helpless. With a little persuasion this was accomplished successfully, and we were able to make the man sit on the road while we called the provincial police to look after him and his truck.

Sad to say, a great deal of our Christian effort in days gone by has consisted of pounding fenders, breaking glass and scratching paint. Many of us have been waging war against the trucks of this world, and have done little to dislodge the power that is in the driver's seat. Our quarrel is not with the systems that are rampant in the world. It is with Satan.

We do not send our missionaries to North Africa to fight the Mohammedans. We send them to fight Satan who is in the driver's seat of Mohammedanism. We do not send our missionaries to New Guinea to cut down the jungles. We send them to cut down the power of Satan who has been in the driver's seat for generations. We do not send our missionaries to Continental Europe to destroy Communism. We send them to destroy the power of Satan that is in the driver's seat of Communism.

Would to God that we could remember! When we pray, the battle is not against "flesh and blood" but against "principalities and powers". When we give, the battle is not against "flesh and blood" but against "principalities and powers". When we go, the battle is not against "flesh and blood" but against "principalities and powers". The struggle is not against *systems* but *Satan*.

CHAPTER IV

NOT CIVILIZATION BUT CHRIST

FROM THE BIBLE

"But if our gospel be hid, it is hid to them that are lost: In whom the god of this world hath blinded the minds of them which believe not, lest the light of the glorious gospel of Christ, who is the image of God, should shine unto them. For we preach not ourselves, but Christ Jesus the Lord; and ourselves your servants for Jesus' sake. For God, who commanded the light to shine out of darkness, hath shined in our hearts, to give the light of the knowledge of the glory of God in the face of Jesus Christ. But we have this treasure in earthen vessels, that the excellency of the power may be of God, and not of us" (2 Cor. 4: 3–7).

CHAPTER IV

NOT CIVILIZATION BUT CHRIST

THE purpose of the missionary is not to take *civilization*, to the heathen, but *Christ*.

Perhaps one of the greatest dangers in all missionary enterprise is to turn from evangelism to education, from preaching Christ to promoting civilization. Instead of concentrating upon turning men from the broad way to the narrow way, we have a tendency to spend our time trying to change men from the Indian way to the British way, from the Oriental way to the American way, or from the African way to the Scandinavian way. The Apostle made it clear when he wrote to the Corinthians: "For we preach not ourselves, but Christ Jesus the Lord" (2 Cor. 4: 5).

The task of the missionary in Africa is not to put clothes on the African. His task is to tell the African about Christ while he is still naked. When we go to the Aboriginal of the great desert of Australia's interior, it is not our duty to teach the native to eat roast beef and Yorkshire pudding instead of roasted grub worms. The Christian is not called to minister in Japan in order that he may teach the Japanese to sit on chairs rather than mats and stools. His call is to take Christ to the Japanese while he continues to sit on his mats and stools. God has not commissioned us to forsake home and friends and go to China to teach the Chinese people to sing four-part American harmony to the rhythm of the American range. Our commission is to take Christ to the Chinese people while they sing their own type of harmony to their own brand of rhythm.

The obligation is not to take hot dogs to the Andes, hamburgers to the jungles, afternoon teas to the islands, or woollen clothes to the tropics. The obligation of the Great Commission is to take the message of Jesus Christ to the peoples of the world and let them develop their own variety of Christian civilization, and because of climatic conditions, geographical differences, and racial origins, the results may seem quite strange to us.

The ideal of most missionary societies to-day is to establish an indigenous church in their fields. By this they mean a church that is supported and manned by the national Christians. However, even where this is the objective, in many cases the missionary does his best to see to it that the native's church is a replica of the Baptist, Anglican, Presbyterian, or Methodist church in which he was reared back home. On most mission fields the churches and their congregations are rough duplicates of European churches, and often the foreign workers have never thought that the native's mind and culture and surroundings might demand an entirely different sort of organization and order of service.

The force of the indigenous church can be lost to a large extent if it is too English, too American, too foreign for the native. "We preach not ourselves, but Christ Jesus the Lord." The Commission is not to take *civilization* to the heathen, but *Christ*.

CHAPTER V

NOT MINOR BUT MAJOR

FROM THE BIBLE

"And as he sat upon the mount of Olives, the disciples came unto him privately, saying, Tell us, when shall these things be? and what shall be the sign of thy coming, and of the end of the world? And Jesus answered and said unto them, Take heed that no man deceive you . . . this gospel of the kingdom shall be preached in all the world for a witness unto all nations; and then shall the end come" (Matt. 24: 3–4, 14).

CHAPTER V

WORLD evangelization should not be treated as a *minor* endeavour, but as the *major* enterprise of the Church.

Most Christians associate the word "missions" with things that are unimportant, inferior, or uninteresting. We think of little groups of ladies drinking afternoon tea and cutting up bandages; church basements cluttered with an array of clothes; household articles that are no longer useful in this country being sold at ridiculous prices; coloured slides of far-away places—many of which cannot be seen because of the poor photography or inadequate projection equipment; moving pictures that produce more headaches than heartaches because very often they have been taken by rank amateurs from the backs of elephants or fast-moving trains; and people whom we conclude have gone to the foreign field because they were not capable of doing an adequate job at home.

These things do not represent true missions, but unfortunately have become associated with missions. It is little wonder that in the average church, missions have been relegated to one small female department of the work.

In The Peoples Church, to avoid these unjust accusations of real missionary work, we choose to use the expression "world evangelization", and the moment it passes our lips we think of concentrated effort, sacrificial giving, vivid pictorial presentation of the greatest battle ever fought, well-trained men and women who could make an adequate mark for themselves in the homeland, and a united campaign in which every department and organization of the church has joined. This is true only because world evangelization has been put in its proper place—not a minor department but the major enterprise.

Every year we have a Conference on World Evangelization. Call it a Missionary Convention, a World Vision Crusade, or World Conquest Rally. During this period we concentrate on missions to the exclusion of everything else that we may be doing. Most churches do this for every other department of their work, but not for missions. Time is set aside for evangelistic crusades. A week is blocked out for the annual Bible Conference. Special speakers are brought in to conduct a prophetic series. Daily Vacation Bible School is held for the children; but there is no concerted effort to promote world evangelization.

An occasional Missionary Sunday, an isolated missionary offering, or a few missionary speakers throughout the year, will never make the people of any church realize that the task of world evangelization is of vital importance. There must be a time when everything else stops, and all the machinery of the church is converted and used on the missionary production line.

The Time

The Conference on Evangelism should be scheduled during the best time of the year. If we hold it when the snow is falling, or the farmers are working, or the people are on their vacations, we are admitting that it is not really important. We have relegated it to a season that is not good for any other kind of meetings. Whenever it is held, it should extend for at least eight days and in some areas it is profitable to go on for two or three weeks.

Counter-attractions

It is vitally important that no other official activity be carried on in the church during the Missionary Conference. There should be no other meetings of any kind. Practices should be eliminated completely or at least reduced to the bare necessity. Class executive meetings can be held during some other week, and of course, no organization of the church would even dream of holding any sort of social activity during the one period of the year when the rest of the church is concentrating upon meeting the needs of dying people.

The Organization

There are many ways that a Missionary Convention can be organized. I am going to mention the things that we have found successful in the work of The Peoples Church. This is not the only method, but it is one that has been tested and proved.

The Speakers

Every session of the convention should feature one outstanding missionary speaker. He may be a missionary, a pastor who has led his people in a great missionary programme or a gifted deputational worker. When we choose a speaker in The Peoples Church, we must have a man who has been gifted by God to reach a large crowd with his message, his presentation must be attractive to the people, and he must have a strong voice so that they can hear what he has to say.

There are many excellent missionaries who are very poor public speakers. As a matter of fact, we have learned that it is possible for a missionary to be invaluable on the foreign field but a poor deputational worker in the homeland, and sometimes the most outstanding deputational worker does not make a good missionary.

If the convention lasts for a full week or more, it is often a good plan to change the main speaker every three or four days.

The Missionaries

It is difficult to conduct a Missionary Convention without missionaries. The more missionaries there are in a convention, the more missionary atmosphere there will be. If the main speaker is not a missionary himself, it is vitally important that missionaries who are home on furlough are invited to the convention so that they can be kept before the people and mingle with them. Apart from any platform work that they may do, the personal contact of missionaries with the people of the church is invaluable.

The New Recruits

One of the greatest sources of stimulation toward missionary giving is the presence and testimonies of new recruits. Almost every society will have candidates for the mission field who have already been trained and are prepared to go. If an opportunity is given for these to be presented to the congregation and bring brief words of greeting and personal testimony, the people will become tremendously interested in doing their part to send them on their way. The new recruits are not only an incentive to missionary giving but will prove to be a tremendous source of inspiration for missionary volunteering on the part of the young people.

The Pictures

Pictures give the people an opportunity to see the work as well as hear about it. We have used three different kinds of pictorial presentation: (i) sound motion pictures with a dramatic missionary story; (ii) sound motion pictures with a documentary commentary; and (iii) 35 mm. coloured slides.

The Christian film companies and the missionary societies themselves have produced many fine dramatic films on world evangelization. These are usually the most interesting to the people, and sometimes they can be instructive. The documentary type film does not attract as large a crowd, but has more of an educational value. Increasing rapidly in popularity are the 35 mm. coloured slides, with which a good speaker can tell a much more complete story than can be presented through any motion film with a sound track.

The chief type of pictures to guard against are those that have no spiritual message, and those which foist poor photography upon innocent congregations. It is just as useless to show pictures which cannot be seen properly as it is to present a speaker who cannot be heard.

The Music

Most churches would not hold an evangelistic campaign without bringing a special speaker and some sort of musician. We are just as careful to plan a good spiritual musical programme during the missionary week as we are for any other special effort we have. It is not necessary for all of the music to be strictly of a missionary nature as long as the congregation concentrates on the great missionary hymns. The special numbers can be chosen from any of the Gospel songs that will add inspiration to the services.

The Programme

In The Peoples Church, we limit the main speakers to twenty-five minutes in every service. This gives ample opportunity for any concise missionary address, and leaves sufficient time for the special music and the pictures. We limit the length of the films to thirty minutes, and if one of the pictures we have scheduled runs longer than this, we cut it down by starting well into the film or stopping before it is finished. Most films have an introductory section that can be left out if necessary, and some films have as many good stopping places as the average sermon.

Every night we present either new recruits or the missionaries or both, depending on the number present. We limit them to about one minute each, and sometimes control this by putting their minute in the form of an interview.

The Exhibit Room

During a Missionary Convention, the people of the church should receive as complete a missionary education as possible. The speaker, the missionaries, the new recruits, and pictures all contribute towards this, but perhaps the best area of education is the Exhibit Room. We ask all of the Missions which are represented to set up a booth in our minor auditorium. There they have an opportunity of displaying their curios and distributing their free literature. We close each service early enough to give the people time to go back to the Exhibit Room and talk with the missionaries, look at the curios, and take the literature.

The Mottoes

Our main auditorium is decorated for the convention with the mottoes that have been used of God to inspire missionary endeavour. Here is a list of some of those which we have found helpful—

"You must go or send a substitute"—*Oswald J. Smith.*

"Anywhere, provided it be forward"—*David Livingstone.*

"If God wills the evangelization of the world, and you refuse to support Missions, then you are opposed to the will of God"—*Oswald J. Smith.*

"Attempt great things for God, expect great things from God"—*Wm. Carey.*

"A man may die leaving upwards of a million, without taking any of it upwards"—*Wm. Fetler.*

"Why should anyone hear the Gospel twice before everyone has heard it once"—*Oswald J. Smith.*

"If Jesus Christ be God and died for me, then no sacrifice can be too great for me to make for Him"—*C. T. Studd.*

"Give according to your income lest God make your income according to your giving"—*Peter Marshall.*

"The prospects are as bright as the promises of God" —*Adoniram Judson.*

"Now let me burn out for God"—*Henry Martyn.*

"Yet more, O my God, more toil, more agony, more suffering for Thee"—*Francis Xavier.*

"The Church which ceases to be evangelistic will soon cease to be evangelical"—*Alexander Duff.*

"Oh for a hundred thousand lives to be spent in the service of Christ"—*George Whitefield.*

"You have one business on earth—to save souls"—*John Wesley.*

"This generation can only reach this generation"—*Unknown*.

"Only as the Church fulfils her missionary obligation does she justify her existence"—*Unknown*.

"The light that shines farthest shines brightest nearest home"—*Unknown*.

"We can give without loving, but we cannot love without giving"—*Unknown*.

"Not how much of my money will I give to God, but, how much of God's money will I keep for myself?"—*Unknown*.

"The supreme task of the Church is the evangelization of the world"—*Unknown*.

Conclusion

Let the whole Church put world evangelization where it belongs. It is not a by-product but the product. It is not a department but the united effort of the entire organization. It is not a preliminary bout but the main event. It is not a side show but the feature attraction. It is not a lane in the country but the main street of the city. It is not a pilot boat but the battleship. It is not a skirmish but the main thrust of the battle. World evangelization should not be treated as a *minor* endeavour but as the *major* enterprise of the Church.

CHAPTER VI

NOT INDEFINITE BUT IMMEDIATE

FROM THE BIBLE

"My meat is to do the will of him that sent me, and to finish his work. Say not ye, There are yet four months, and then cometh harvest? behold, I say unto you, Lift up your eyes, and look on the fields; for they are white already to harvest. And he that reapeth receiveth wages, and gathereth fruit unto life eternal: that both he that soweth and he that reapeth may rejoice together. And herein is that saying true, One soweth and another reapeth. I sent you to reap that whereon ye bestowed no labour; other men laboured, and ye are entered into their labours" (John 4: 34–38).

CHAPTER VI

NOT INDEFINITE BUT IMMEDIATE

THE work cannot be left until the *indefinite future*; it must be done in the *immediate present*.

Our opportunity of obeying the commands of God or of reaching the world on His behalf is often referred to in the Bible as a time of harvest. Jeremiah, the prophet, lamented the fact that the Jewish nation had missed a time of harvest during one period of their history: "The harvest is past, the summer is ended, and we are not saved" (Jer. 8: 20). When Jesus had talked to the woman at the well and sent her back to her village, she returned bringing with her the entire population of the place. The disciples had just come back from the same town and brought nothing but food. It is not always the best qualified religious leaders that do the greatest work for God. However, as the woman was coming across the fields with the people following, Jesus said to His disciples, "Say not ye, There are yet four months, and then cometh harvest? behold, I say unto you, Lift up your eyes, and look on the fields; for they are white already to harvest" (John 4: 35).

Jesus was not referring to the corn harvest. It was still green in the fields. It would not be white unto harvest for another four months. He was speaking of the human harvest that was following the woman to the well and to Jesus.

Only one of two things can happen to a harvest. It can be gathered in when it is ready, or it can be left to be destroyed by the elements.

So it is with the harvest of men's souls. There is a time when it can be gathered in, but there is a time when "harvest is past, the summer is ended." For more than a quarter of a century now our people in Toronto have been made aware of the urgency of the task by a constant repetition of a short motto—"This generation can only reach this generation."

This generation of Christians is responsible for this generation of heathen, and if we fail to give them the Gospel they will be lost. It is impossible for us to reach the last generation. They have long since died. It will be impossible for us to reach the next generation. By the time they are alive we will be with the Lord. That means that the only group of people we can reach is our own generation of heathen, and we are the only ones who can reach them.

This is our task, but in the face of the statistics it seems impossible. Over half the world's population have not yet been evangelized. There are approximately forty-four million people added to the world's population every year. Of these only about two million ever hear the Gospel. Almost forty-two million of the souls born into the world every year never hear the message. How then can we hope to cope with the problem?

The missionary faces the same insurmountable obstacle the moment he arrives on the field. He mans a small station, with heathenism walling him in on all sides. He ministers in a heathen city for thirty years, and has been unable to get as far as the next village with the Gospel. The demands are exhausting, the multitudes are bewildering, and the opposition is devastating. But the Great Commission remains, and it must be carried out.

Obviously, the flesh and blood missionary alone can never finish the task. Does that mean the Lord has given us an impossible job? A generation ago it might have seemed so, but not today. The ingenuity of the twentieth-century man has made world evangelism a possibility within one generation. The missionary has at his disposal today the tools that will enable him to fulfil the command.

Aircraft

Modern aviation makes it possible for us to reach the most remote parts of our world within a matter of days. Less than twenty-five years ago it usually took months for a man to get to the mission field, and then at great peril to his life, as he made his way up treacherous rivers, through dense jungles, and over dangerous mountain trails. The same invention transports invaluable food supplies, medical needs, and equipment for his work. When necessary, the missionary who is seriously ill can be flown to adequate hospitals where competent doctors can prolong his years of usefulness on the field.

Medicine

In the earlier years of missionary enterprise the worker was weakened and often lost as a result of diseases that he was not able to cope with or ward off. Modern medicine has changed the picture entirely. Vaccinations, inoculations, and miracle drugs have made it possible to work in the midst of disease-ridden areas and to maintain a much higher standard of health and thus a longer period of service.

Radio

No one will ever be able to estimate accurately the tremendous impetus to the spread of the Gospel that has been given by the use of radio. When Dr. Clarence Jones first intimated that he intended to set up a broadcasting station in the heart of the Andes Mountains in Equador and send the Gospel around the world from that one point, people thought it was not only impossible but rather foolish.

Today, every Christian knows the outcome of that venture of faith. HCJB is only one of several similar stations that are strategically located to carry the Gospel to scores of countries. Radio broadcasting combined with correspondence courses have enabled the potential of one missionary to be multiplied many times over.

Records

As a result of the efforts of Gospel Recordings and other similar groups, the new missionary can become an effective evangelist long before he has learned the language himself. He goes into a tribe with a small spring-operated record player under his arm, and, equipped with Gospel messages in the language of the people, he can gather a group of natives about him and fascinate them with his miracle-machine that speaks their language. Not only are the people fascinated, but—although they may not at first be aware of it—they are hearing, perhaps for the first time, the message of God's love.

Literature

Aircraft, medicine, radio, and records, together with many other modern devices, have certainly multiplied and accelerated the work of every flesh-and-blood missionary. However, with all of these methods combined the present staff of missionaries, or even a greatly increased staff, could never reach the entire world with the Gospel in our generation. Our hope of getting the task completed lies in literature—the Word of God and the Gospel message printed in the language of the people.

The world is rapidly becoming literate. A short time ago we had concluded that one million every month were learning to read. With the vast literacy programmes of the governments of China and India now in full progress we can safely assume that nearly one million people every *week* are becoming literate.

Dr. Frank Laubach has developed a system whereby he can go into a tribe of completely illiterate people and in a matter of weeks teach the head man of that tribe to read their own language. The chiefs in turn teach the other men to read, and *they* teach their families. Thus in a matter of a few months an entire tribe can become literate. Millions of men and women, as a result of this process, are now able to read. A generation ago this was impossible.

Now we are faced with the challenge of a million new literates a week, fifty-two million a year who are looking for something to read. The Communists have taken up the challenge and are smearing the world with tons of literature. The Roman Catholics have realized their opportunity and are flooding the world with their literature. The false cults are awake to this new channel of propagating their religion and are using it to the utmost.

The Communists boast that they conquered China with the printed page. Between 1928 and 1950 Jehovah's

Witnesses produced more than half a billion pieces of literature in eighty-eight different languages and had propagated them in over a hundred different countries. Since 1950 they have accelerated the work of their presses tremendously, and as a result, you can find their literature throughout the world.

A man who has just learned to read is not particular what he reads, just as a hungry man does not care what he eats. If necessary he will scrounge in a garbage heap to satisfy the hunger of his body. Are millions of souls learning to read only that they may feed their minds from the garbage heaps of the world's literature, or will the Christian Church take up the challenge, buy up the opportunity and put Gospel literature in their hands?

The potential for reaching the world in our generation through the printed page is tremendous, but every other religion has the same avenue of approach open to it. In most cases the battle is won by the man who gets there first. If we fail to gather the harvest, the enemy will come in and destroy it. We can reach the world in our generation, but we must act in the immediate present. We cannot leave the task until the indefinite future.

Marilyn Bell

In the year 1954 a little sixteen-year-old girl made herself the most famous, and possibly the most beloved girl in Canada, by swimming the thirty-two miles across Lake Ontario. No one had ever done it before, but Marilyn Bell was successful. The following summer she made a successful attempt at swimming the English Channel. In the summer of 1956 she conquered the Strait of Juan de Fuca between Vancouver Island and the mainland.

When she was making her bid for the English Channel in the summer of 1955, the entire Canadian Broadcasting Corporation network, along with many independent radio stations, remained on the air through the hours of the night and gave a stroke-by-stroke account of her swim. I listened to it with a great deal of interest, as did thousands of other Canadians.

The first ten hours of the swim were completed at a rapid stroke of more than sixty to the minute, but when she was within sight of the Cliffs of Dover the tides began to carry her back as fast as she swam forward. For nearly two hours she continued to swim but made no progress. Finally, by increasing her stroke to an almost incredible rate, she began to move again, swam through the tides and set foot on the beach in England.

The next day the Canadian newspapers were full of the swim. One official observer on the English side, who had seen many Channel swims, was quoted as having commented while Marilyn was having difficulty with the tides: "If Marilyn is not ashore by ten-thirty tonight, when the tide goes out, her chances of completing the swim will be about nil."

As I read this quotation I thought of another channel, the channel of heathenism. I thought of the multitudes that were trying desperately to make their way across it and plant their feet on the shores of salvation. But, alas, they do not know the way! And I thought I could imagine the comment of some Heavenly observer, "If someone does not show them the way, the tides will go out, and when the tides go out their chances of being saved will be about nil."

And the tides are going out. Already the tide of Communism has carried one-third of the world's population almost beyond reach. Every day that we live the tide of death takes 120,000 souls out of the world. Of these, probably more than half are taken from the channel of heathenism into an eternity without God. It is essential that we realize that the task of world evangelism cannot be left until the *indefinite future*; it must be done in the *immediate present*.

PART II

THE MONEY THAT MOVES THE MACHINERY

"How shall they preach, except they be sent?"

CHAPTER VII

NOT MEN BUT MONEY

FROM THE BIBLE

"For there is no difference between the Jew and the Greek: for the same Lord over all is rich unto all that call upon him. For whosoever shall call upon the name of the Lord shall be saved. How then shall they call on him in whom they have not yet believed? and how shall they believe in him of whom they have not heard? and how shall they hear without a preacher? And how shall they preach, except they be sent?" (Rom. 10: 12–15).

CHAPTER VII

NOT MEN BUT MONEY

THE bottle-neck of world evangelism is not *men* but *money*.

Missionary work involves two groups of people, the goers and the senders. The Bible makes this quite clear. "How shall they preach, except they be sent?" (Rom. 10: 14, 15). To suggest that everybody ought to be a missionary on the foreign field is just as foolish as to say everyone should be in the army and sent overseas during a war. Every nation realizes that it takes two kinds of people to wage a successful war. There must be the manpower on the firing line, but there must also be those who are able to send him there, keep him there, and supply him with ammunition. It usually takes scores of people at home for every one that is at the front.

So it is with the war of world evangelization. The soldier of the Cross on the mission field cannot operate without the soldier of the Cross in the business office and in the home. Even the Apostle Paul had to be sent by the church at Antioch and supported by many of the other churches in order to carry on his missionary work. God does not give everybody the privilege of working in the front lines of the battle. Some are called to maintain the supply lines at home where there is not much glamour or glitter or glory or adventure.

The problem that confronts us is this: the task is not being done. Millions of people have not yet seen their first missionary. Where is the bottleneck? Do we lack men, or do we lack money?

We lack money. The men are available. Never has there been a generation when there were so many well-trained young people anxious to do the will of God. Our Bible Schools and Christian Colleges in North America alone are turning them out every year by the hundreds, and a poll of almost every evangelical school will reveal that a good percentage of these young people would like to go to the mission field. The sad truth of the matter is that only a very small percentage of them actually reach their goal. Briercrest Bible Institute and Prairie Bible Institute in Canada have about the highest percentage of their graduates on the mission field, and that amounts to only twenty per cent and less.

Where is the break-down? Why is it that more young people who want to go to the field do not get there? Let me give you the answer with a personal illustration. In 1951 some of the Youth for Christ leaders came back from the Orient to the conference at Winona Lake, Indiana. I shall never forget that year. The need in Formosa and Japan and the Philippine Islands was tremendous, and the door was wide open. The men from these places spoke many times, and always their plea was the same: "We need men for the Orient. I have come home to find men."

That year they found the men—not just a few, but hundreds of them, young people whose hearts were moved by the appeals. I saw them as they made their way forward in the Billy Sunday Tabernacle indicating their desire to go. I was one of them. Rev. John Henderson was another. We had been holding evangelistic campaigns throughout Canada and the United States for several years, treading on the toes of others who were doing exactly the same thing. At that time we were not really needed at home. Here was an opportunity to go where we were needed desperately.

Since the appeal had been made particularly for teams that included a preacher and some kind of musical ability, my song leader and I constituted exactly what they wanted. We applied, and we were accepted by the Council of Youth for Christ International to go to the Philippines. What a thrill it was!

To this day neither John Henderson nor I have set foot on the Philippine Islands as missionaries. Why? Youth for Christ asked us to do what any missionary society must ask—raise the money for your fares and your salaries, and we will send you. I did not know how to raise the money, and it was an enormous amount, much more than the average missionary had to raise to go to the field. My father had made it a policy not to do anything special financially for his own family that he could not do for others. Thus what The Peoples Church could have done would have been only a drop in the bucket.

We were just two young men among hundreds of others, most of whom to this day have not left the shores of America. In this case the bottle-neck was not men; it was money.

For seven years I was the Associate Pastor of The Peoples Church, and since January of 1959 I have been the Pastor. Our office is in contact with the mission field every day. Almost every week we receive a letter from one of the faith missions that reads something like this: "We have three young men who are accepted candidates for the mission field. Can you help us with their support?" Or like this: "We have a young couple who are urgently needed on the field. We lack their personal support. Could your people help us?"

Sometimes we are able to answer in the affirmative, but in the majority of cases we have to refuse. So far our people have only supplied enough funds to contribute to the personal support of about 350 missionaries. Gradually we are trying to increase that number, but we have almost reached the saturation point of giving in The Peoples Church.

What does this mean? Simply that almost every faith missionary society, and some of the denominational missionary societies, have accepted candidates at home because they do not have sufficient funds to send them to the field. Hold a missionary convention, and most organisations can send a half-dozen new recruits to appeal to the people every year.

Have you ever noticed the number of young people that are going about the country doing deputational work? There is a steady stream of them at our prayer meetings, our young people's organisations, our Sunday Schools, and other church gatherings. What are they doing? They are trying to raise their support, hoping and praying that some business man, some Bible class, some church will say, "We'll send you to the field." And most of them waste—yes, positively waste— six months, a year, and in some cases several years waiting for God's people at home to be sufficiently stirred to send them.

Someone says that it is good training for the field to go about in the homeland trusting God for their support. Such sheer nonsense! These are young people that have already gone through the training of a Bible School and its discipline, and usually before we ever see them they have spent weeks in training at the mission's candidate school. After all that, we let them waste their time trying to raise money—and few of them know how to do it—in our Christian countries, when we know that 120,000 souls are dying every twenty-four hours, and most of them without Christ.

Obviously, the break-down is not men; it is money. We have the men. Every church sees the men as they go through month after month, and the main reason we see them is that we have not supplied the money.

In my evangelistic work throughout the world I usually set aside a night to preach on missions. At the close of the service I extend an invitation in these words: "How many young people thirty years of age and under, will say: If God wants me to be a missionary, I will be one. Come forward and stand at the front of the auditorium." I have done this all over the world, and almost inevitably every Christian young person in the building will stand up, come forward, and declare: If God makes it clear to me that He wants me to be a missionary, I'll be a missionary.

Suppose I were to make an appeal for funds to the business-men in the same audience in these words: "How many businessmen will stand up and say: If God wants me to give Him fifty per cent of my income for foreign missions, I will do it." What sort of a response would I get? One man, half a dozen men, or a score of men out of an audience of two thousand people? More than likely there would be no response whatsoever. We expect our young people to lay down their lives for God, but most of us are not willing to lay down our bank accounts.

We have the men, but we do not have the money. If we had the money, we could get the task completed in our generation. The bottle-neck of world evangelization is not *men* but *money*.

CHAPTER VIII

NOT CASH BUT CREDIT

FROM THE BIBLE

"For as touching the ministering to the saints, it is superfluous for me to write to you: For I know the forwardness of your mind, for which I boast of you to them of Macedonia, that Achaia was ready a year ago; and your zeal hath provoked very many. Yet have I sent the brethren, lest our boasting of you should be in vain in this behalf; that, as I said, ye may be ready: Lest haply if they of Macedonia come with me, and find you unprepared, we (that we say not, ye) should be ashamed in this same confident boasting. Therefore I thought it necessary to exhort the brethren, that they would go before unto you, and make up beforehand your bounty, whereof ye had notice before, that the same might be ready, as a matter of bounty, and not as of covetousness. But this I say, He which soweth sparingly shall reap also sparingly; and he which soweth bountifully shall reap also bountifully. Every man as he purposeth in his heart, so let him give; not grudgingly, or of necessity: for God loveth a cheerful giver. And God is able to make all grace abound toward you; that ye, always having all sufficiency in all things may abound to every good work" (2 Cor. 9: 1–8).

CHAPTER VIII

NOT CASH BUT CREDIT

THE method is not *cash* but *credit*.

We very seldom are able to pay for the big, important things in life with cash. In most cases, if it were not for credit we could not have many of the things that are ours.

We buy our homes on credit. If we were to wait until we had saved sufficient cash to pay for a home completely, we would wait in vain. It would take three thousand pounds or ten thousand dollars to buy the average home. How many of us have ever been able to accumulate that much cash at one time? It would be an impossibility for most of us, but the average person has a home. How do we do it? We go to a bank, a mortgage company, or sometimes an individual, and borrow the money, and promise to pay it back in monthly instalments during the next twenty or twenty-five years.

We do the same thing when we buy a car, and many people buy a great many other things in the same way. If you were to take from the average American or Canadian family the things he is buying on credit, you would leave him in the street with no furniture and often without the clothes on his back.

What are we actually doing when we take a mortgage on a home or finance a car? We are obligating ourselves for a period of months or years to a bank so that we can have the buying power of a large sum of money. Why do we do it? Because we think a home and a car are important. We are willing to obligate ourselves to pay for the important things of life.

The question I want to ask now is this: How important do you consider the work of God, the task of world evangelization? Have you ever taken out credit in the Bank of

Heaven? Have you ever obligated yourself to God to such an extent that you have been able to do something really big? As long as you try to pay for missions with the cash on hand, the job will never be done. No one has that much cash; but if you will obligate yourself to God, in faith, over a period of twelve months, and promise to give a specified amount month by month during that period, you will be amazed at what you can do.

We receive an offering for missions once a year in The Peoples Church. It is not a cash offering, nor is it a pledge offering. It is not cash, because our people could never give enough cash at any one time to enable us to meet our obligations. It is not a pledge, because a pledge is usually made to a church, and eventually someone from the church may try to collect it.

It is a faith-promise offering. Our missionary envelope reads: In dependence upon God I will endeavour to give month by month . . . and there is a place to mark the monthly amount on the side of the envelope. We write to everyone who has filled in an envelope and tell them how and where to send their money, but from that point on the transaction is between the individual and God. We never check up to see if the amount has been paid.

Thus the people have not made a pledge to the church. They have made a faith promise to God, and they trust Him to enable them to pay it. This is the kind of offering the Apostle Paul received from the Corinthians. He sent men "beforehand" to make up a "bounty", and he urged them to give, "Every man as he purposeth in his heart" (2 Cor. 9: 1-8). He did not ask for cash. He asked them to make a decision in their own hearts about how much they would be able to give between the time the messengers were sent and the time he arrived.

This is the great New Testament principle of giving that we have tried to put across to our people in The Peoples Church. This is why so many of them have been able to support their own missionary. With cash they could never do it, but with a faith promise they can.

The Support of a Missionary

The support of a missionary can be broken up in many different ways. That is why you get such a variety of figures when you ask how much it costs. Generally speaking the support of each individual missionary is divided into "personal" and service". The personal support is the salary the man receives on the field. The service support may include a great many other things depending on the financial policy of the particular mission. Usually it includes furlough allowance, passage money for the furlough, upkeep on the mission station, supplies necessary for the work, and other items, all of which are a part of the cost of keeping the missionary on the field. If a man is married, his wife gets the same allowance and service support. If they have children, they receive an allowance for each child.

Thus the answer to your question might be two hundred pounds (six hundred dollars) or two thousand pounds (six thousand dollars). Both answers would be correct. The first is the average salary of the missionary on the field. The second is the personal and service support of a man and his wife with several children. Some of the older denominations pay much higher salaries than the Faith Missions.

In The Peoples Church we assume responsibility for the average personal support of all of our missionaries. This amounts to approximately two hundred pounds (six hundred dollars) a year. In some missions the amount is higher. In some it is lower. We do this for several reasons. It puts the support of a missionary within the grasp of the average Christian. When an individual or a class in the church support their own missionary in this way, it makes world evangelization a personal matter. They know their missionary. They can correspond with him and pray for him as an individual. This is an advantage to both the givers and the missionary.

This method also spreads the interest of our people around the world, instead of concentrating it on one field. It keeps the world before the people, and as a result they are not localised in their vision. They have a world vision.

However, even the personal support of a missionary could never be assumed by the ordinary business man if it had to be done on a cash basis; but when he looks forward a year, and makes a faith promise to God to pay a specific amount month by month, just as he pays the mortgage on his home, he discovers that he can accomplish things for God that otherwise would be an impossibility.

Have you ever made a faith promise? Have you ever managed to do something big for the cause of world evangelization? Have you ever dreamed of supporting your own missionary? You can do it, if you will make a faith promise to God. Obligate yourself to Him, just as you have obligated yourself to the bank. When it is time to pay your bills, pay your bill to God first. Take it off the top of your income at the beginning of the month. If you take it off the bottom there will be nothing left. One reason we have not done the job before now is that we have paid all the other bills first and have had nothing left for God.

Jesus said, "But seek ye first the kingdom of God, and His righteousness; and all these things shall be added unto you" (Matt. 6: 33). Most Christians have never put that promise to the test. From our files in The Peoples Church we could produce story after story of men and women who have made a promise to God in faith, often not knowing where the money was going to come from, and in a miraculous way God has sent it in.

We cannot finish the task with cash. We can finish it on credit. The method is not *cash* but *credit*.

CHAPTER IX

NOT CHARITY BUT CHOICE

FROM THE BIBLE

"Wherefore, if God so clothe the grass of the field, which today is, and tomorrow is cast into the oven, shall he not much more clothe you, O ye of little faith? Therefore take no thought, saying, What shall we eat? or, What shall we drink? or, Wherewithal shall we be clothed? (For after all these things do the Gentiles seek:) for your heavenly Father knoweth that ye have need of all these things. But seek ye first the kingdom of God, and his righteousness; and all these things shall be added unto you" (Matt. 6: 30–33).

CHAPTER IX

NOT CHARITY BUT CHOICE

GOD does not want our *charity* but our *choice*.

For nearly two thousand years we have been giving God our charity. We give Him charity when it comes to prayer. Most Christians decide on their prayer time by checking their day's activities, marking off the periods that are taken up with important things, and giving God what is left over. Instead of setting aside the best time of the day for God, we have given Him charity. Prayer time is the period that is no good for anything else—charity.

During the special missions that come to our city or town we give God our charity. We think of all the things we must do each night of the week, and whatever night is left over we go to the mission. In this generation seldom does a Christian anticipate the special mission and then deliberately block off those nights on his calendar for God, eliminate all less important projects, and give God the entire week. Oh, what a blessing there could be in your town if a few hundred Christians and their families would give a week or a fortnight to God for evangelism! When it comes to local evangelism we give God what is left over—charity.

The Old Piano

Quite often in our church in Toronto the telephone will ring and at the other end the voice of some good Christian lady will say: "We are in the process of buying a new grand piano for our home, and I wonder if you could use our old one in the church?" Of course, we never say no. We have old pianos all over the church, and we are very grateful for them; but I have yet to hear a voice at the other end of the telephone line say, "We were about to buy a new grand piano for our own home, but we have decided that the old upright will do for us. Could we make a gift to the church of the new grand?

The Old Instruments

When Dr. Paul Roberts was about to leave Toronto for his work at HCJB, a local doctor called my father saying that he had a set of rather old medical instruments. He wondered if they would be any use on the mission field. I happened to be home the day Dr. Roberts came to my father's house to look at the instruments. I remember the expression on his face as he told how out-dated some of them were, but quickly added that he would be thankful for them on the mission field. How different it would have been if some Christian doctor had offered to equip the young missionary doctor with a complete set of brand new instruments.

These are not isolated cases. This happens in every church every year, and in the large churches almost every month. What does it mean? Simply that we are trying to do the work of God on charity. We are willing to give Him whatever we cannot use ourselves—charity.

We do the same thing with our money. We do not give God the "first fruits", the best lamb; we give Him the money we have left over after we have used all we want to use on ourselves.

The Indian Baby

The young man had just arrived in India. He was walking along the banks of the Ganges. He passed an Indian woman. In her arms was a fat, healthy baby girl. By the hand she was holding an anaemic little boy. It was obvious that he would not live very long. His body was contorted by disease. The young missionary looked and passed by. An hour later he returned. There stood the same woman. The frail little boy was still there, but the fat healthy baby girl was gone.

The young man spoke, "I saw you here a short time ago and there were two children. One was a very fine baby girl. What happened to her?"

"I threw her into the Ganges. It is a part of my religion."

"But if you were forced to sacrifice one of your children, why did you not keep the healthy child and throw the disease-ridden boy into the Ganges? He would not have lived long at best."

The heathen woman drew herself up proudly, and before she turned to walk away with the emaciated boy, she said with a note of fervour in her voice, "Sir, our gods demand the best."

That is an old story that has been told many times, but I do not know of an incident that points out the contrast more vividly. We give our God charity. The heathen give their gods choice.

The Haitian Church

When I was in Haiti in 1949 I had the privilege of preaching to the Haitian Christians at the annual Christian's Convention of the West Indies Mission. I spoke several times each day to audiences of over six thousand people. I shall *never forget them*. They had a prayer meeting every morning at six o'clock. Two thousand of them came to pray.

They had come to the convention in many different ways. Some had ridden long distances on their little donkeys. Some had come by *commione,* or Haitian bus. When they load a bus in Haiti, it is filled to overflowing! I took pictures of some of the buses as they arrived. There were people inside, on the top, hanging on both sides, and some were walking ahead and others behind. They arrived singing the Gospel hymns in their own language. Most of the people walked to the meetings. I met a number who had walked through the valleys and over the hills more than a hundred miles, and after the convention they walked home again.

While they were there the women slept on the benches in the tabernacle. The men slept out on the ground. They cooked their meals over small fires built on the hard sun-baked dirt of the fields.

At the close of the conference the missionaries took a survey of their offerings for the past year. The average

Haitian farmer in that district makes about twenty or twenty-five American dollars a year. That is all the cash these people ever see. When the survey was made, to my amazement I learned that they had given over ten thousand American dollars for the support of their own churches and for world evangelization. That year some of their money was sent as a missionary gift to one of the American Bible Societies.

I was put to shame as I was confronted with the sacrificial giving of these people who had lived in the darkness of Voodooism only a few years before. Nowhere in the Christian countries had I ever seen such giving. Where did they learn it? They learned it in their heathenism. Pagan religions demand the best of their followers. They are not content with charity. They must have the choice, and they get it.

For generations we have been trying to do the work of spreading the Gospel around the world with the charity of Christians. The majority of our missionary work has been carried on with the left-overs of God's people. Old pianos, old medical instruments, old clothes, old books, old cars, and old money—money that we have decided can be of no legitimate use to us.

What a transformation there would be if we would keep the charity for ourselves and give God the choice! God does not want our *charity* but our *choice*.

CHAPTER X

NOT TITHE BUT TOTAL

FROM THE BIBLE

"For the kingdom of heaven is as a man travelling into a far country, who called his own servants, and delivered unto them his goods . . . Moreover it is required in stewards, that a man be found faithful . . . I beseech you therefore, brethren, by the mercies of God, that ye present your bodies a living sacrifice, holy, acceptable unto God, which is your reasonable service" (Matt. 25: 14; 1 Cor. 4: 2; Rom. 12: 1).

CHAPTER X

GOD does not ask for our *tithe* but our *total*.

There is nothing wrong with tithing. If some Christians did not tithe, they would give practically nothing to the work of God. However, the tithe was simply a minimum percentage set by God for the Jews. The tithe was by no means the ideal of giving even in Old Testament days. There were all sorts and varieties of offerings given to God by the people over and above their tithe. The tithe they owed God as a matter of business. It was an automatic thing. The offerings were given for special occasions and extra projects, to a large extent out of gratitude to God for His blessings.

In the New Testament the principle is obviously changed. Not only does the tithe belong to God, but also the man's body and everything he possesses. "I beseech you therefore, brethren, by the mercies of God, that ye present your bodies a living sacrifice, holy acceptable unto God, which is your reasonable service" (Rom. 12: 1). The Christian's body is the property of God and the temple of the Holy Ghost. If we have dedicated our lives to God, then everything that is in our possession belongs to the Lord.

Jesus makes that quite evident in His parables about the man travelling to the far country and the nobleman going away from his property. In both cases the servants were left with money, but it was not theirs. They were allowed to use it while the master was gone, but they were required to give an account of it when he returned (Matt. 25 and Luke 19).

The Christian is, throughout the New Testament, referred to as a steward: "Moreover it is required in stewards, that a man be found faithful" (1 Cor. 4: 2). A steward is never the owner. The property and the money he may control is not his; it belongs to his master. The Christian does not own his house, his car, his food, his bank account, or even the clothes on his back. Everything he has is God's. God has permitted him the use of these things as a steward, but the Bible tells him unmistakably that there is going to be a day of reckoning when he will have to give an account to God of what he has done with God's property.

The average Christian gives, asking this question: "How much of my money will I give to the Lord?" Of course, this is the wrong way to put the question. We cannot give God any of our money. We do not have any money. It is all God's. The New Testament way to ask the question is this: "How much of the Lord's money will I keep for myself?"

What we give is not as important as what we have left after we have given. It was not the widow's mite that pleased Jesus. It was almost without value. It was the fact that she had deprived herself to give the mite. It was "all that she had" (Mark 12: 41–44). When Jesus "sat over against the treasury", he was not interested in what the people gave, but in what they had left. The large gifts of the rich men did not impress Him in the least, because they gave "of their abundance", and they had more than enough left for themselves. The widow gave out of her poverty and had nothing left. The sacrifice is more important than the gift.

Most Christians have given something toward world evangelism, and as we face the coming year we will probably give again. How much will we give? There are four possibilities. First, we may decide to give nothing. If we do, we are virtually casting a ballot for the recall of every missionary from the field and the closing of our mission stations. If every Christian did nothing, that is exactly what we would have to do.

Second, we may choose to give less than we did last year. This would indicate that we have adopted the doctrine of retreat. Bring home some of the workers, close up some of the stations, and do less on all fronts. If every Christian were to give less, the missionary societies would have no other choice but to retreat.

Third, we may determine to do the same this year as last. That would mean that we approve of holding the ground we have already captured, but that we do not wish to gain any more ground. Man the present fields, but do not do any trail-blazing or pioneer work. If all Christians maintained their present level of giving, there could be no advance. We would have to content ourselves with digging in and holding.

Finally, we can endeavour to give more this year than we have ever given before. We can trust God to enable us to do something bigger than we have ever had the privilege of doing. This would prove that we believe in advancing. Enter new fields, establish new stations, reach the unreached peoples, and move into the territory of the enemy. It will only be when God's people around the world move forward in their giving that the missionary will be able to move forward with his work.

The tithe will never be sufficient to enable us to advance and complete the task in our generation. It will take a total, all-out effort on the part of God's people, that will involve personal sacrifice, or the job will never be done. God does not ask for our *tithe* but our *total*.

F

CHAPTER XI

NOT PRIVATION BUT PRIVILEGE

FROM THE BIBLE

"Who then is Paul, and who is Apollos, but ministers by whom ye believed, even as the Lord gave to every man? I have planted, Apollos watered; but God gave the increase. So then neither is he that planteth any thing, neither he that watereth; but God that giveth the increase. Now he that planteth and he that watereth are one: and every man shall receive his own reward according to his own labour. For we are labourers together with God: ye are God's husbandry, ye are God's building" (1 Cor. 3: 5–9).

CHAPTER XI

WORKING with God is not a *privation* but a *privilege*. I have yet to hear a missionary talk about the sacrifice he has made to go to the field—and I have been in the company of missionaries from all over the world all my life. The people at home sometimes speak about the privations of the missionary's life, but never the missionary himself. If he is a real missionary, called by God—and I have met some mistakes on the mission field, people who were obviously not called to the task—he does not consider it a privation to be on the foreign field; he thinks of it as a privilege. Most missionaries are among the happiest of Christians, and would not exchange places with the people at home for any amount of money.

However, there is no doubt about it that relative to the giving of the Christian who has not been called to the front lines, the missionary has made a great sacrifice. He has forsaken home and friends to become an ambassador in a foreign land for the cause of the Gospel. He has given himself to God. The tragedy is that those of us who have been left behind have not begun to match the sacrifice of the army at the front. The missionary may know something of sacrifice. Most of us know nothing about it. Privation for the sake of the Gospel is a stranger in our experience.

Fried Chicken and Sterling Silver

I was asked to dinner in the home of a very lovely Christian lady in a great American city. Several missionaries were there with me. We had been conducting a missionary convention in one of the local churches. The hostess was quite apparently wealthy. It was a beautiful home, furnished magnificently. We sat down to a table set with sterling silver and burdened with food fit for a banquet.

The dear woman had just returned from Palestine, and in the course of her tour she had seen the orphans of the Holy Land—frail, hungry, pathetic. She described them to us, and it was obvious that she had a great burden for them. I shall never forget what she said, and the situation in which she said it: "My heart went out to those hungry little boys and girls who had never heard the Gospel. Oh, that we could tell them about Jesus! Mr. Smith, would you please pass the fried chicken." And as I passed the chicken a tear ran down her cheek and fell on a sterling silver spoon.

I do not condemn this dear soul, because she is just one of thousands of Christians in the homeland who sit in the lap of luxury and talk about the need of the heathen. Here we are in the Christian countries surrounded on all sides by things we do not need, and we seem to feel that Almighty God should feel highly honoured because we have given Him a few dirty dollars or paltry pounds.

The people in The Peoples Church in Toronto, Canada, probably give as much to the cause of world evangelization as any congregation in the world. The total is in the vicinity of three hundred thousand dollars. This is considered a great example of what can be done. However, when it comes to real sacrifice, we have not begun to scratch the surface. The luxuries of our people alone represent an enormous amount of money.

In Canada nearly everyone has a "coffee break" in the morning and afternoon. We have more than two thousand adult givers in the church. Coffee costs ten cents a cup. If our adherents would add the same amount to their missionary giving as they spend for their daily "coffee breaks" the total in a year's time would be forty-eight thousand pounds or one hundred and forty-six thousand dollars.

If we were to add to that the cost of radios, rugs, jewellery, clothes, etc., that are in the luxury class, the sky would be the limit. I am not trying to say that we should give up our "coffee breaks" or afternoon teas, nor that we should do without the luxuries of life, but I do think we should do at

least as much for the cause of Christ as we do for the cause
of our own comfort.

Suppose someone does see his responsibility to God as far
as his giving is concerned, and makes a contribution that
costs him something. Has he really sacrificed? Has he suffered
a privation? Of course not. Working with God is not a
privation either on the going end or the giving end.

Certainly God does not need man. He could have done
the work alone, or He would not be God. God does not
need you in the foreign field to help Him with His work.
God does not need my little bit of money to help Him carry
out His purpose. He owns the cattle on a thousand hills and
the diamonds in a hundred mines. The glory of the Gospel is
not that God needs us, but that in His love and graciousness
He has given us the privilege of working with Him. "For
we are labourers together with God" (1 Cor. 3: 9).

If Queen Elizabeth II were to dispatch a message to me to
the effect that she would like me to leave my home and friends
and come over to Great Britain to help her with some project,
what would my reaction be? Would I count the cost carefully,
consider the sacrifice involved, and rather reluctantly answer
in the affirmative? No. Without a moment's hesitation, I
would board the first plane to Buckingham Palace and get
on with the job. Any British citizen would deem it a privilege
to work with the Queen.

The Queen will never give me the privilege of helping her
with a project, but the thing that humbles me is the fact that
the King of Kings has enlisted my help in the greatest project
in the world. He tells me I can go. I can pray. I can give
my money. It would almost be blasphemous to think of it
as a privation. Working with God is not a *privation* but a
privilege.

PART III

THE MARKS THAT MAKE THE MISSIONARY

"If God be for us, who can be against us?"

CHAPTER XII

NOT RELIGION BUT REGENERATION

FROM THE BIBLE

"Finally, my brethren, rejoice in the Lord. To write the same things to you, to me indeed is not grievous, but for you it is safe. Beware of dogs, beware of evil workers, beware of the concision. For we are the circumcision, which worship God in the spirit, and rejoice in Christ Jesus, and have no confidence in the flesh" (Phil. 3: 1–3).

CHAPTER XII

NOT RELIGION BUT REGENERATION

THE origin of the missionary is not *religion* but *regeneration*.

The third chapter of Philippians is probably the best life-story of the world's greatest missionary that we can find anywhere in the Bible. The whole chapter is based on the personal experience of the Apostle Paul.

In verses two and three of this life-story chapter we find a keen analysis of the essential differences between the religous man and the regenerated man. This is the essential starting point of every missionary. Verse two is a description of a religious man—the kind of man the Apostle Paul was *before* his experience on the Damascus road. Verse three is a description of a regenerated man—the kind of man Paul became *after* his experience on the Damascus road. Verse two is not only a warning to young Christians to beware of the Judaizers, or religious people, but it is a picture of what the Apostle was himself at the time.

Paul describes the religious man with three words—dogs, workers, and concision. He describes the regenerated man with three other terms—in Christ, no confidence in the flesh, and circumcision. In Christ as opposed to dogs. No confidence in the flesh as opposed to workers. Circumcision as opposed to concision.

When you know the story of the Apostle Paul you realize that in these two verses he is painting a picture of what he was and what he became. Verse two is Paul before the Damascus road, verse three is Paul after the Damascus road. Verse two is Paul as a religious man, verse three is Paul as a regenerated man. These verses contrast what the Apostle was *before* and what he became *after* the Damascus road, in three ways.

Lost and Saved

The Apostle as a religious man was lost, but as a regenerated man he was saved.

He describes the religious people of his day by the use of the word "dogs", and of course Paul knew better than anyone else that he had been one of them himself. The word "dog" was used by the Jews as a term of contempt for the Gentiles. Jewish people in Paul's day, and Jewish people today, are very particular about their food. Certain foods, according to law, are clean, while others are unclean. Some food can be eaten by the Jew, but some cannot be eaten. When we see the word *kosher* written on the front of certain shops, it does *not* mean that the food sold under that name is more highly seasoned; it simply means it is ceremonially clean.

The Gentile people of the world have never been particular about their eating habits. They eat any kind of meat in any form or combination, without any discrimination whatsoever. When the Jew looked at the Gentile and observed the fact that he ate both clean and unclean food, he immediately classed him with the dogs of the day. They were literally scavengers. There was no such thing as canned dog-food or chlorophyll dog biscuits. The dogs simply ate from the garbage heaps or from the left-overs and waste of their masters' tables. Jesus spoke about dogs eating the crumbs which fell from the master's table.

As a result of this similarity between the Gentile and the dog, as far as eating habits were concerned, the Jew began to call anyone who lived outside of Judaism a dog.

Theologically, in the New Testament, the term "dog" was adapted and applied to anyone who was outside of Christ— not a believer. The Book of Revelation in speaking about heaven, describes the people who will not be there with this old Jewish expression: "for without (heaven) are dogs." Thus the word dog for the Jew referred to anybody outside of Judaism, and the word dog for the early Christians referred to anyone outside of Christ.

When Paul warns the Philippians to beware of mere religion, he refers to the religious people of his day as dogs. "Beware of dogs." Avoid the man who is religious but who is outside of Christ, or lost. The Apostle Paul was numbered among that group at one time himself. He was a dog. He was religious but he was lost.

As opposed to the religious man whom he describes as a "dog" he now describes the regenerated man with the use of the phrase "in Christ". The Apostle, as a religious man, was a dog, but as a regenerated man he was in Christ. As a religious man he was lost, but as a regenerated man he was saved.

The regenerated man is "in Christ" in the sense that he is in the family of the Lord: "As many as received Him, to them gave He the power to become the Sons of God, even to them that believe on His name" (John 1: 12).

The regenerated man is in Christ in the sense that he is in communion with the Lord: "Behold, I stand at the door, and knock: if any man hear my voice, and open the door, I will come in to him, and will sup with him, and he with me" (Rev. 3: 20).

The regenerated man is in Christ in the sense that he is in love with the Lord. "We love Him, because He first loved us" (1 John 4: 19).

Finally, the regenerated man is in Christ in the sense of that mystical union which can only be partially described in such terms as the branch in the living vine, stones forming a part of a living building, and members as an intricate part of a living body.

Works and Grace

The Apostle as a religious man depended upon his works for salvation; but as a regenerated man, he had no confidence in the flesh.

Paul describes the religious people of his day with the word "workers". He admits the fact that the Jewish people were religious workers, but he combines the word "workers" with the word "evil". They were "evil workers". This again is what the Apostle Paul had been himself before his regeneration. No one could refute his claim of having been an ardent religious worker. He had been so desperately zealous in his attempts to oppose the work of the early Christian church in the name of religion, that he had "made havoc" of it.

The regenerated man goes about preaching the Gospel and sowing wheat. The religious man works ardently preaching another gospel and sowing tares in the same field. That is exactly what these people were doing in Paul's day. He was sowing the wheat; they were sowing the tares. He was working, and they were working; but his work was building the Kingdom of God, and theirs was attempting to destroy the Kingdom of God. They were working, but they were working toward an evil end.

Possibly the greatest enemy of the early Christian church was to be found in the efforts of the Judaizers to move the young Christians from the simplicity of their faith in Jesus Christ back to the form, ceremony, and ritual of religion. From that day to this the powers of darkness have been attempting to do the very same thing. If the devil can succeed in robbing the Christian of his childlike faith in Jesus Christ, and cause him to rely upon the form and ceremony of mere religion, then he will have accomplished his purpose.

The reformation in Luther's day was necessary because the church had lost its belief in salvation by faith, and had become a huge, cold, lifeless, religious body. When Luther protested, he protested against this loss of simplicity; and when the Reformers moved out, they moved back to the Bible doctrine of salvation by grace through faith.

The spiritual and moral reformation which took place under the ministry of John Wesley was necessitated by the fact that the Church of England had begun to stress its form and ceremony and ritual to such an extent that simple faith in Jesus Christ and holiness of life had become obscured. John Wesley moved out of the Church of England in order to emphasize these truths once again.

When the Puritans came to America in the seventeenth century they came for exactly the same reason—that they might be free from the ritual, form and ceremony of the powerless church of their day, and worship God scripturally.

The great temptation of every new Christian group is to grow up and become dignified and gain ecclesiastical recognition. Usually this involves the building of a religious machine, the formation of an elaborate liturgy, and an over-emphasis upon the scholastic standing of its clergy. All of these things, of course, have their place in the church; but history has proved many times over that with growth and maturity and the development of a machine there is the danger of lack of power, dead formality, modernism, and worldliness.

Most of the regular denominations of our day were born in the midst of revival fires; but in a great many cases the devil has been successful in sowing the tares of ritualism, formalism, and scholasticism to such an extent that the fire has been put out. When this takes place, the Spirit of God steps over the walls of these organizations and moves on to work among the minority groups who have remained faithful to the Word of God.

In contrast to the religious man who is simply an "evil worker", Paul speaks about the regenerated man as having "no confidence in the flesh". He has no confidence in the origin of the flesh. The Apostle was writing to a group of people who were proud of their racial origin. The same group in Jesus' day boasted to Him, "We have Abraham to our father," whereupon Jesus replied, "God is able of these stones to raise up children unto Abraham". They were proud of the fact that they were Jews. They not only boasted of their racial origin, but they were beginning to depend upon it for their salvation. Jesus made it absolutely clear that the fact that these people were the children of Abraham was no credit to them. God could raise up children to Abraham from the stones or the dirt upon which they stood.

The Apostle Paul had superior racial background of which to boast, than the majority of the people to whom he was writing; and despite all of it he was able to say, "I have no confidence in the flesh".

The regenerated man has no confidence in the ability of the flesh. "Not by works of righteousness which we have done, but according to his mercy He saved us." The Christian knows that no amount of praying, giving, working or worshipping has resulted in his salvation. He has no confidence whatever in the ability of the flesh, but he has complete confidence in the efficacy of the finished work of Jesus Christ on Calvary's Cross.

Concision and Circumcision

The Apostle as a religious man practised an empty formality, but as a regenerated man he worshipped God in the spirit.

Paul refers to the religious people of his day as the "concision". Actually they were Jewish men who had in their bodies the mark of circumcision. Circumcision simply means that a man is set apart as a worshipper of God. It means he is in contact with God. The virtue of circumcision, however, is not the mark but rather the reality for which the mark stands. The important thing is not the circumcision, but contact with God.

That is true in any sphere of life. The emblems of an officer in the army are not important in themselves; they are valuable only because they represent something that is important. The crown on the shoulder of a Canadian soldier does not make him a major. He wears the crown because he *is* a major. The important thing is not the crown—it is the rank for which the crown stands.

The religious people of Paul's day still had the mark of circumcision, but they had lost the reality for which that mark stands; they had lost their vital contact with God. Therefore, Paul does not call them the circumcision; he calls them the concision.

Concision means a mutilation of the flesh which has no real significance. The bodily mutilations we have seen in pictures of heathen tribes, among whom missionaries are working today, could only be called concisions, because they do not mean anything of eternal importance. They are nothing more than mutilations of the flesh.

If a Jewish man has lost his contact with God, his mark of

circumcision has become nothing more than a mutilation of the flesh, or a concision.

In verse three Paul describes himself and other Christians as the real circumcision. Some of the early Christians were Jews, and actually had in their bodies the literal mark of circumcision. However, there were many of them that had come from the pagan world, and of course did not have the actual mark of circumcision; but Paul describes all of them as the circumcision, because as believers they possessed the reality for which the mark of circumcision stands. They were in vital contact with God. They were true worshippers of God through Jesus Christ; and so Paul says, "We are the circumcision, which worship God in the spirit."

The great danger of the Christian religion is to emphasize the symbols of our faith to such an extent that we lose sight of the reality for which they stand. Beautiful church buildings are designed to carry the eye of man heavenward and thus make it easier for him to worship God, but it is quite possible to become so enthralled with the beauty of our church buildings that we lose our contact with God. Then, of course, the symbol becomes meaningless. The cross is another symbol that has done a great deal to draw the attention of the child of God to the sacrifice of His Saviour, but it is quite possible to so emphasize the cross as a symbol of religion that we lose sight of the Lord Jesus Christ and our obligation to Him. The ordinances of communion and baptism and dedication become meaningless in themselves unless we are in personal contact with the Lord Jesus Christ.

The essential virtue of the Christian religion is not to be found in its symbols but in its Saviour; and when the symbols, or the marks, become the important thing and we lose the reality for which they stand, then they are nothing more than mutilations and we are little more than the concision.

The man who is merely religious is lost. He is an evil worker. He belongs to the concision. The man who is regenerated is saved. He has no confidence in the flesh, and he belongs to the circumcision. The origin of the missionary is not *religion* but *regeneration*.

CHAPTER XIII

NOT GOODNESS BUT GODLINESS

FROM THE BIBLE

"Though I might also have confidence in the flesh. If any other man thinketh that he hath whereof he might trust in the flesh, I more: Circumcised the eighth day, of the stock of Israel, of the tribe of Benjamin, an Hebrew of the Hebrews; as touching the law, a Pharisee; Concerning zeal, persecuting the church; touching the righteousness which is in the law, blameless. But what things were gain to me, those I counted loss for Christ. Yea doubtless, and I count all things but loss for the excellency of the knowledge of Christ Jesus my Lord: for whom I have suffered the loss of all things, and do count them but dung, that I may win Christ, And be found in him, not having mine own righteousness, which is of the law, but that which is through the faith of Christ, the righteousness which is of God by faith: That I may know him, and the power of his resurrection, and the fellowship of his sufferings, being made conformable unto his death; If by any means I might attain unto the resurrection of the dead" (Phil. 3: 4–11).

CHAPTER XIII

NOT GOODNESS BUT GODLINESS

T HE robe of the missionary is not *goodness* but *godliness*. There are many other ideas that are incorporated in verses four to eleven of the third chapter of Philippians, but as a whole they present one major theme—Paul's spiritual robe before and after he became a Christian. If we were to think of verses seven and eight as the pivot point of a balance, hanging on one side would be verses four, five and six—describing Paul's goodness as a man; and on the other side would be verses nine, ten and eleven, indicating Paul's Godliness as a Christian. Verses seven and eight are the pivot point of the balance, because there is registered Paul's evaluation of the two.

As he considers what was his before he was apprehended by Christ on the Damascus road, he is able to boast of a great deal more than the average religious man of his day. He lists seven reasons for boasting—four which were his by inheritance, and three which were his by accomplishment.

Circumcision

The moment Paul said "circumcised the eighth day" he elevated himself in the minds of his Jewish readers above the heathen, the proselytes, and the Ishmaelites. The heathen world had no claim to the ordinance of circumcision, and therefore had none of the privileges of the covenant that lay behind it. The proselytes were circumcised, but always remained inferior because it was done at the time of conversion. The Ishmaelites were also circumcised, but not until the thirteenth year. Thus the Jew who could say "circumcised the eighth day" was considered spiritually superior.

Stock

The Apostle then added that he was "of the stock of Israel". Other nations had descended from Abraham and Isaac and could claim the distinction of circumcision, but only the Israelites had descended from Jacob and could claim the promise of God's covenant with Jacob. Jacob had wrestled all night until God had blessed him in a singular way and declared him to be a Prince with God. Israel was the highest title of God's ancient people. To use this name was indeed a privilege devoutly to be wished, and Paul had that privilege.

Tribe

Paul was further elevated in the Jewish mind when he said he was "of the tribe of Benjamin". This was important because it was from this tribe that Saul emerged as the first king of Israel. The tribe of Benjamin never wavered from their allegiance to the house of David, and it was in the territory of the tribe of Benjamin that the Holy City of Jerusalem was built.

Education

The fourth thing that was his by inheritance was a Hebrew education. He was able to say that he was "a Hebrew of the Hebrews". This indicated that Paul was reared in a home which had maintained all of the Hebrew customs and spoke the Hebrew language. This was not true of all the Israelite homes, and certainly not of all the Jewish homes; but there were in Paul's day a few families that were so utterly orthodox that they adhered to the oldest of Jewish customs and conversed with one another in the Hebrew tongue. Paul came from such a home. He was a real Hebrew.

Accomplishments

The first four distinctions were his by inheritance. Now he mentions what was his by choice.

First: "As touching the law, a Pharisee." Everyone knew that this was the strictest religious sect of the day. The Pharisees were undoubtedly closer to the Kingdom than most of the other organizations of that period. They were the most spiritual and the most orthodox. Possibly that is why Jesus so often upbraided them in particular. "Whom the Lord loveth He chasteneth." Many of the early converts to Christianity came from among the Pharisees. Nicodemus, that very zealous ruler of the Jews, was a Pharisee.

Second: "Concerning zeal, persecuting the church." Paul was not only a Pharisee, but a very active one. So zealous was he that he delighted in contending for his faith by persecuting the Christians because they constituted a threat to the whole Pharisaical system.

Third: "Touching the righteousness which is in the law, blameless." According to the Jewish standard of righteousness the Apostle Paul was able to say that he was perfect. He was sacrimonially perfect because he had observed all of the ordinances. He was doctrinally perfect because he knew and believed the law.

No wonder he was able to look the religious world of his day in the face and say, "If any other man thinketh that he hath whereof he might trust in the flesh, I more."

Having said these things regarding his robe of human goodness, Paul then turned to a consideration of his robe of Christian Godliness.

"And Be Found in Him"

To be a Christian means to be in Christ. As the branch is in the vine and draws its life from the vine, so the child of God is in the living body of Christ and draws his life from Christ. If we are born again we are in Him now, at the last day, and always.

To be in Christ means to be clothed in the righteousness of Christ, "Not having my own righteousness which is of the law, but that which is through the faith of Christ; the righteousness which is of God."

A few years ago I visited a sheep ranch in the hills of New Zealand. Near the homestead we noticed a small enclosure where there was one large ewe with a very small lamb—only a few days old. What caught my eye was the fact that the lamb was skipping about the pen wearing an overcoat. Not only did he have his own fine covering of wool but he had another complete lamb's skin over the top of his own. At first I thought he was just a Canadian lamb trying to keep warm in New Zealand. But then the rancher told me the story: His mother had given birth to triplets. She was not able to take care of all of them, and this one was left. The ewe had lost her own lamb, but she would have nothing to do with this strange-smelling orphan. The rancher had taken the skin from her own dead baby and wrapped it around the motherless lamb, and the problem was solved. Now the bereaved mother smelled the coat of her own baby, and began to take care of the orphan who was wearing it. The lost lamb had found a mother by virtue of the coat he was wearing.

There is probably no better illustration than this of what the Apostle Paul meant when he said: "And be found in Him, not having mine own righteousness . . . but that which is through the faith of Christ." The Christian finds favour in the eyes of God because he is clothed in the righteousness of Jesus Christ.

How hopeless would be our condition before God if we had only the merits of our own righteousness to present! But how wonderful to realize that when we are "found in Him" we are clothed in the spotless robe of His righteousness, and God looks upon us favourably because of Jesus.

"That I May Know Him"

Not only does the Christian abide in Christ—as the branch in the vine—but he knows Him as a bride knows the bridegroom.

There are three ways that we may know a person. We may know someone who does not know us. I know Queen Elizabeth II, but she does not know me. Or we may know someone who does know us by virtue of a formal introduction. When I am introduced to a man, I know him and he knows me. I know his name. He knows my name. I know his position in life, and he may know mine. Most of our acquaintances are this kind.

However, there are always one or two people in the world whom we know as we do not know others. A man knows his wife in this way. He has loved her and spent many years in intimate fellowship with her, and as a result he knows her. This knowledge involves feeling, sympathy, and understanding. This is the kind of friendship that stems, not from an introduction, but from a long period of close communion.

This is what is involved in the word the Apostle uses here: "That I may know Him." Not that I may read about Him or be introduced to Him, but that I may know Him as an intimate Friend. This knowledge of the Lord is not the result of reading and study but of communion and fellowship. It is not so much a knowledge of the head as of the heart. The Christian who thus knows Him can say:

And He walks with me, and He talks with me,
And He tells me I am His own,
And the joy we share as we tarry there,
None other has ever known.

Christ for Paul was not only his life—he was in Him—but also his Friend—he knew Him.

"And the Power of His Resurrection"

The Apostle had already experienced the resurrection power of the Lord on the Damascus road, but he realized that this was but an earnest of the power that would some day raise his body from the grave.

The same power that brought life back into the body which the Roman soldiers laid in Joseph's tomb has been experienced by every Christian. The resurrection power of the Lord Jesus

Christ has worked within our hearts the miracle of the new birth. That power has brought us from death in our trespasses and sins unto life in the Lord Jesus Christ. That power has transformed our lives from darkness to light. That power has made of us "new creatures" and caused old things to pass away that all things might become new.

It is because we already know the resurrection power that we can look forward with confidence and hope to the glorious resurrection of our bodies that still lies in the future.

"And the Fellowship of His Sufferings"

What a thought! The sinner has the privilege of sharing in the sufferings of his Saviour.

We can fellowship in the external sufferings of our Lord. He lived a sinless life and as a result He was hated, rejected, and persecuted by the world long before He went to the cross. As we live a holy life for God, we too will suffer the slings and arrows of a world that hates righteousness; but even while men revile us and persecute us and say all manner of evil against us falsely, we can remember that it is for His sake; and as we bear it, we fellowship with Him in His sufferings.

We can also fellowship in His internal sufferings. He knew no sin, but in His humanity He waged a continual war against the temptations of the world, the flesh and the devil. "He was tempted in all points like as we are, yet without sin." What a consolation in the midst of Satan's onslaughts to know that we are sharing in the same kind of battle which Jesus fought before us. We have fellowship with Him in His sufferings.

Finally, in a minor degree, we can have a sympathetic fellowship with Him in His sufferings on the cross. No human being can ever share the burden that He bore or feel the pain that He felt or know the heartache that He knew. We can only look at the cup which He drained to the dregs. We can only stand on the edge of the storm through which He passed. We can only imagine the abyss which He probed to the depths.

But as we contemplate His death on the cross we can sympathize to some extent and thus know the fellowship of His sufferings.

"Being made Conformable unto His Death"

Perhaps the Apostle is looking forward to his own death, and because of his relationship to the cross of Christ he is prepared for it or conformed to it. More likely he is talking about the crucifixion of the flesh to which he had become conformed. He had reckoned himself dead unto self and sin, that he might live unto Christ and righteousness. He amplified the truth in Galatians when he said: "I am crucified with Christ: nevertheless I live; yet not I, but Christ liveth in me." The Christian conforms to the death of his Lord in so far as he dies to himself and Christ lives His life through him.

"Attain unto the Resurrection of the Dead"

"If by any means" does not express doubt but humility. Paul considered himself the "chief" of sinners, and for him to realize that he would have a share in the final resurrection of the righteous seemed almost too good to be true. The sheer glory of the truth humbled him.

"I might attain" brings in the thought of a journey. To attain means to arrive at the end of that journey. Paul always thought of the Christian as a pilgrim in a foreign land, traveling towards his home. There are trials and tribulations along the way, but if we are "found in Him," there is resurrection and glory at the end of the road.

Paul had already experienced resurrection power in his regeneration, and he anticipated the same power in his body which would one day make him victorious over death and the grave. For the Christian, the heavenly life begins here. The life of faith is the beginning of the life of glory. Both consist of union with Christ. They differ only in degree but not in kind. The life of faith with all the hindrances of the world and the flesh removed, climaxes in the life of glory.

Evaluation

On one side of the balance is Paul's robe as a man—his inheritance and his accomplishments. On the other side is his robe as a Christian. In verses seven and eight we have Paul's own evaluation.

He considered his inheritance and accomplishments, but in the light of the glory of his possessions in Christ they began to shrink in his estimation until all that was left on the balance was a heap of "dung". Opposite the robe of his human goodness he wrote the words, *no profit*. "Yea doubtless, but I count all things but loss."

Then as he contemplates the glory and the blessings and the privileges that were his when he was clothed in the robe of Christian Godliness, he could think and write only one word, "excellent".

The Christian may have "suffered loss", but his profit is greater than his loss because he has gained Christ. The robe of the missionary is not *goodness* but *Godliness*.

CHAPTER XIV

NOT COMPLACENCY BUT CONCENTRATION

FROM THE BIBLE

"Not as though I had already attained, either were already perfect: but I follow after, if that I may apprehend that for which also I am apprehended of Christ Jesus. Brethren, I count not myself to have apprehended: but this one thing I do, forgetting those things which are behind, and reaching forth unto those things which are before, I press toward the mark for the prize of the high calling of God in Christ Jesus. Let us therefore, as many as be perfect, be thus minded: and if in any thing ye be otherwise minded, God shall reveal even this unto you" (Phil. 3: 12–15).

CHAPTER XIV

NOT COMPLACENCY BUT CONCENTRATION

T HE attitude of the missionary is not *complacency* but *concentration*.

Whether you have actually competed in a "miracle mile" or simply run in a "three-legged race" against your neighbour in a Sunday School picnic, you are familiar with the terminology of the racecourse. The people to whom Paul was speaking were familiar with the sport of racing, and when he used this analogy of the Christian life in the third chapter of Philippians, they knew exactly what he was talking about.

The first great missionary made it clear that if we are to be successful in any kind of race, whether it be against flesh and blood on one of the racecourses of this world or against principalities and powers on the spiritual racecourse, certain attitudes are essential.

These can be described by the use of three simple words —dissatisfaction, obliteration, and concentration.

Dissatisfaction

Dissatisfaction is the first step toward spiritual progress. Paul says, "Brethren, I am dissatisfied; 'I count not myself to have apprehended!'"

He was not dissatisfied with his physical or material state of prosperity. He was one man who had learned in whatsoever state he found himself, physically or materially, therewith to be content. In this letter to the Philippians he makes it clear that he had learned how to abound and he had learned how to be abased. He could get along with a great deal or he could get along with very little. He was not dissatisfied with his material or physical position, but he was dissatisfied with his moral and spiritual progress.

The springboard of advancement, even on the level of every-day life, is dissatisfaction. There is no progress without it. It was only because someone became dissatisfied with living in a cave that today we live in houses. It was because the American people became dissatisfied with the Pony Express that their letters are carried by air. Because people became dissatisfied with being clothed in the skins of animals in their raw state, we find ourselves clothed as we are. If the world had never become dissatisfied with the horse and buggy, we would not be driving automobiles and riding trains and buses today. It was because women became dissatisfied with the arduous task of using a scrub board with which to do their washing, that today we have produced the automatic washing machine. Dissatisfaction is the first step toward progress on any level.

In the spiritual world, the principle is the same. If there is no dissatisfaction spiritually, there will never be any progress spiritually. It is absolutely essential that there burn within the breast of every Christian a thorough-going dissatisfaction with his own moral and spiritual advancement.

The important thing is not the victories we have already won but the victories that still need to be won—not the ground we have already gained but the great area that still lies within the hand and the power of the enemy. If we dwell upon the blessings we have already received, there will be no incentive to reach out for the multitude of blessings that are still to be claimed. If we rest after we have gone the first mile, we will never go the second mile. If we relax after we have won one soul, we will never win a score of souls. If we are content when our church is supporting five or six missionaries, we will never attempt to support more. We must focus our attention upon what still needs to be accomplished. This is essential.

Perhaps the greatest blight upon many of our Christian churches and Christian people is the fact that we have gone a little way, we have accomplished something, we have gained ground, we have won a few victories, and we have become satisfied. We have stopped. We are marking time, and in many cases we are stagnating, and pollution and corruption is the result.

Dissatisfaction is essential to Christian progress. If we are to run well for God, there must burn within our breasts a thorough-going dissatisfaction with our present moral and spiritual attainment.

Obliteration

The Apostle says that we must not only be dissatisfied with the present, but we must obliterate the past—"Forgetting those things which are behind."

This means obliteration of the sins of the past. There is a sense in which memory of past sins can keep us in a position of humility before God, but there is another very real sense in which memory of the sins of the past can become a brooding that impedes our future progress. Repentance of sin is one thing. Repining over sin is another. If our sins are confessed, they are forgiven, they are cleansed. If they are cleansed, they are to be remembered against us no more forever. If God forgets, how much more should you and I forget. It is possible to so dwell upon the sins of the past that our possibilities of service and blessing in the present and the future are destroyed. Progress on the racecourse depends upon "forgetting those things which are behind"— obliteration.

There should be obliteration of the failures of the past. There are some Christians who base their hopes for the future on the *statistics* of the past. They failed last year, therefore they will fail next year. They have always lived a defeated Christian life, therefore they always will live a defeated Christian life. In the past they have gone down under the pressure of temptation, therefore in the future they will succumb to temptation. What they have been, they will be. They are basing their expectations for the future on the statistics of the past.

This kind of Christian needs to remember that the power of God can change the course of the statistics. God can transform failure into success. He can change weakness into strength. Defeat can become victory. For the Christian, the future does not depend upon the past. It depends upon the power of God.

Where would some of the great characters of the Bible have been if they had been content to base their hopes for the future on the statistics of the past? The third chapter of the book of Jonah commences this way: "And the word of the Lord came unto Jonah the second time." This was after Jonah's experience with the great fish. If Jonah had been like a great many modern Christian people as he stood on the shores of the sea with his experience of defeat and failure behind him, when God gave him a second opportunity, he would have said: "It's no use. I was called once, and I did not respond. I received a commission to preach at Nineveh, and I turned my back and found a ship going to Tarshish. Find somebody else to fulfil the commission. I am a failure. I always have been a failure, therefore I always will be a failure."

If Jonah had done that, perhaps over 600,000 people in the city of Nineveh would never have received God's message, but Jonah was able to forget the things which were behind. He was willing to obliterate the failures of the past and he moved on toward the city of Nineveh to preach in response to the call of God, with the past behind him.

We all know the result. The Spirit of God fell upon Jonah and transformed his failure into success and his defeat into victory. The city of Nineveh heard God's message and were spared—just because one man refused to base his hopes for the future upon the statistics of the past.

Perhaps the most broken-hearted man in the world at the time of the crucifixion was the Apostle Peter. There he stood in the midst of a worldly crowd, warming his hands over the world's fire and denying that he had ever been associated with his Lord. He was defeated, discouraged, undoubtedly broken-hearted.

Approximately fifty days later, on the day of Pentecost,

the Spirit of the Lord came upon the same man and told him to stand up and preach. Peter might well have said, "Find someone else to do the preaching. I can still remember that day in the upper room when I professed that I would lay down my life for the Lord Jesus if necessary, and yet before the cock crowed the next morning I had denied Him three times. I cannot preach because I am a failure. I cannot answer the call of God because I made a mistake at one time in my life. I cannot rise to a position of leadership because my actions in the past have proved that I am weak and incapable of assuming such a responsibility."

Peter might have talked in this manner, but he did not do it. He was willing to obliterate the past, and the power of God fell upon him in such a way that when he stood to preach that day three thousand men and women responded. Once again God had changed the course of the statistics. God had used a man who had refused to base his hopes for the future on the statistics of the past.

"Forgetting those things which are behind" involves obliteration of the *sorrows* of the past. I have known some Christians to dwell so deeply on the sorrows of the past that they have destroyed the possibility of joy and usefulness in the future. Bereavement has crossed their path, disappointment has found its way into their lives, or sickness and disease have handicapped them, and for years they have been nursing a broken heart. They have refused to be comforted. They have turned their backs upon happiness; they have avoided blessing, and as a result they have been useless to themselves, useless to other people, and useless to God. They have never obliterated the sorrows of the past. If the Christian really believes in the reality of the resurrection, how foolish it is to weep forever at the grave.

The *attainments* of the past should be obliterated. The Christian is not meant to glory in a golden age which is behind, but upon the golden age which is yet to come. The limitless possibilities of the future should be his standard—not the achievements of the past. He should always remember that no matter how much he may have received already, the best is yet to come. For the Christian the best wine is always reserved for the last. The future is the most glorious.

Concentration

It is not enough to be dissatisfied with the present and to obliterate the past. We can do both of these, and yet stand still on the Christian racecourse. The third word must characterize our lives if we are to be successful in reaching the mark. There must be concentration.

Paul says, "This one thing I do." The first foreign missionary was a success because he was a "one track man". He lived for only one thing: that he might be a witness to the saving power and grace of God. That is all! Everything else was secondary to him. He had a singleness of purpose, concentration of life, energy and ability.

Analyse the career of any eminently successful man, and you will discover that whether he be a business man or a professional man, the focal point of his entire life is his work, and everything else is wrapped around it. Everything else is secondary. He lives, eats, breathes, laughs, plays, sleeps and dreams his work. As a result he stands at the top of his bracket. The reason most people do not succeed is that they try to do too many things. Man is only able to concentrate upon one thing. If he does, he succeeds. If he does not, he fails.

The Christian needs to realize that he has been left in the world for only one purpose—that he might be a witness to the saving grace of God. That is why the Christian is a father second, and a witness first. A business man second, and a witness first. A professional man second, and a witness first. A mother second and a witness first. He is in the world to be a witness, and he must concentrate upon fulfilling his calling.

Paul describes the extent of his concentration by the words "reaching forth". When a horse is racing at full gallop, at the end of the course he usually puts on an extra burst of speed in his attempt to overtake his competitors. To do this he has to use all of his reserve energy and power. He stretches his body out to its full extent, holds nothing in reserve, but gives the race everything he has. He is stretching out to win the race.

This is the idea that Paul is putting across in these verses when he uses the words "reaching forth". He is thinking of the racer using that last little bit of reserved energy and power in order to reach the mark. The reason the average Christian does not run as well as he might is that he holds too much in reserve. He has ability which has never been given to God. He has talent which has never been dedicated to the Lord. He has energy which has been dispersed elsewhere. He has brain power that he has concentrated on other things. He has time which has been spent on the world. He has never really stretched out for God. He has never given God everything. He has never exerted that last little bit of energy. He has never used up the reserve.

Paul says that if we are to run well for God we must concentrate upon giving God our very best: "This one thing I do . . . reaching forth unto those things which are before".

The Mark and the Prize

The Christian is running toward the mark, not the prize. The mark, in an ordinary race, is the line of white ribbon at the end of the course. The mark indicates the finish of the race. The concentration of the runner is never upon the prize, but always on the mark. In the Christian race, our objective is not the prize; it is the mark. The mark is not happiness, but holiness. It is not paradise, but perfection. "Be ye holy, for I am holy." The child of God is aiming at that holiness of life and character which will be a constant witness to the world in which he lives of the saving power and grace of God.

We concentrate upon reaching the mark, but it is clear that some day we are to receive the prize. The prize is not given out on the racecourse: the prize is to be given out at the Judge's stand; and if we have run well, there will be a time when we will hear the voice of God calling us higher. In response to the "high calling of God" we will move from the racecourse of life up to the Judge's stand, where we will receive the prize.

We concentrate upon perfect holiness, and we are rewarded by perfect blessedness. We strive toward moral and spiritual perfection, and we are rewarded by eternal paradise. We reach forth to gain the mark, and some day we are called higher to receive the prize.

If you are regenerated, you are on the spiritual racecourse. If you would run well for God, your life must be characterized by dissatisfaction, obliteration and concentration. "Brethren, I count not myself to have apprehended"—dissatisfaction. "Forgetting those things which are behind"—obliteration. "This one thing I do"—concentration. The mark is holiness and the prize is Heaven.

The attitude of the missionary is not *complacency* but *concentration*.

CHAPTER XV

NOT SINNER BUT SAINT

FROM THE BIBLE

"Nevertheless, whereto we have already attained, let us walk by the same rule, let us mind the same thing. Brethren, be followers together of me, and mark them which walk so as ye have us for an ensample. (For many walk, of whom I have told you often, and now tell you even weeping, that they are the enemies of the cross of Christ: Whose end is destruction, whose God is their belly, and whose glory is in their shame, who mind earthly things.) For our conversation is in heaven; from whence also we look for the Saviour, the Lord Jesus Christ: Who shall change our vile body, that it may be fashioned like unto his glorious body, according to the working whereby he is able even to subdue all things unto himself" (Phil. 3: 16–21).

CHAPTER XV

NOT SINNER BUT SAINT

THE example of the missionary is not the *sinner* but the *saint*.

No one is absolutely original. The Apostle Paul re-emphasizes this truth in these verses as he urges the Christians of Philippi to use him, and other people like him, as an example for their Christian lives. He states the same principle in Romans: "for none of us liveth to himself".

The truth set forth is one which the average person is loth to admit. Most people like to think of themselves as original, either in action or thought or word. However, if we analyse life carefully, we will discover that in most cases we are not entirely original.

On May 13, 1940, Sir Winston Churchill made his first address to the British House of Commons as Prime Minister. In that speech he said: "I have nothing to offer but blood, toil, tears and sweat." These words were heralded around the world in the headlines of our newspapers as among the great original statements of our generation. Undoubtedly this was an important thing to say, and the world felt its effect to the full; but most people who are interested in literature realize that John Donne said almost the same thing in the year 1611, and Lord Byron repeated it in 1823. The primary difference between Winston Churchill and lesser people is that he knew when to say it again, and how to adapt it to the crisis at hand; but even Sir Winston Churchill is not absolutely original.

Most of our learning comes as a result of imitating other people. The psychologist calls the people we imitate "models" because in a sense we model our lives after theirs.

This is just as true spiritually as it is physically. Christians imitate other Christians, and a great deal of what we learn spiritually we learn from watching others and patterning our lives after theirs. Of course, we realize that the supreme example of all Christian living is the Lord Jesus Christ Himself. Despite this fact the Apostle Paul recognizes that most Christians will look for help to other people, and to some extent arrive at a pattern for their Christian living from them. These verses indicate two kinds of models whom we could imitate. They could be called the sinner and the saint.

There are five differences between these two, and Paul describes them vividly.

Allegiance

The basic distinction between the sinner and the saint is that one owes his allegiance to Christ, the other to the world. The sinner is described as belonging to a group of people who are "enemies of the cross of Christ". The saint is associated with a group who are called "citizens of heaven", "for our conversation (citizenship) is in heaven."

The man who takes a stand in opposition to the cross, takes his stand with Satan. He is opposed to the work of Christ, he recognizes no obligation to Him, and he is not on his way to Heaven. He owes his allegiance to the arch enemy of the cross, the devil. In vivid contrast to this man, Paul calls the saint a citizen of Heaven. He has knelt at the foot of the cross, he has accepted Jesus Christ as his own personal Saviour, and his name has been written down in the Lamb's Book of Life. He owes his allegiance to Christ.

Objective

The objective of the sinner is to gratify the flesh; "his God is his belly". The objective of the saint is to crucify the flesh. Paul refers to his body as "vile".

The sinner lives to satisfy himself, to fulfil his own ambitions, to cater to his own desires. Appetite is master of the man.

Although the Apostle Paul would be the first to proclaim the fact that his body was "fearfully and wonderfully made" and the temple of the Holy Ghost, he also recognizes that the material of the body are dust and ashes. It is the body that is subject to the diseases and infirmities and sinful desires, which limit the capacity of man to such an extent in this life. In one sense it is the body that drags him down and away from God. With these thoughts in mind Paul condemned his body as vile, and in many instances throughout the Epistles he talks of crucifying the body, or putting it down in order that he may better live for God.

All the endeavours of the sinner are concentrated upon his objective in life—to gratify the flesh. All of the efforts of the saint are concentrated upon his great objective—to crucify the flesh, and as a result let the Lord Jesus Christ live through him.

Sense of Values

The saint weeps over his sins, and the sinner glories in his sins. When Paul describes the life of the worldly man, he is so wrought up about his sin that he says, "I now tell you even weeping." As a Christian, sin is so horrible to him, so destructive, that the very thought of it breaks his heart. Now he describes another kind of person, who revels in his sin; "whose glory is in their shame." The very thing over which one weeps, the other glories in. What makes one ashamed, makes the other proud. What one hates, the other loves.

Sin has so perverted and warped the mind of man that he actually boasts of the things of which he should be thoroughly ashamed. He rejoices over those things about which he should weep. But the godly man is ever conscious of what sin did— it caused Christ to die on the cross. Of what it is doing—it is creating the corruption present in the world today, ruining homes, and blighting lives. Of what it will do—it leads to destruction. This, of course, makes the saint hate sin, and even the thought of sin almost crushes him.

Interest

The concern of the sinner is this world, and the concern of the saint is the next world. The sinner not only lives in this world. He is attached to it. His roots are in it, and he is a part of it. He minds "earthy things". He is living in this world, and for this world. His attention is focused upon the home life, the business and the pleasure of the world.

The saint is living in the world, but his hope lies beyond it. He is "looking for the Saviour". He is in the world, but not tied to the world. He is on the world, but not rooted in the world. He does his task here, but his home is over there.

The same ocean-going vessel can carry immigrants leaving their homeland and citizens returning to their homeland. The first group will weep when they say farewell; the second group will rejoice. The immigrant leaves behind him all that is dear to him. His roots are in the old world. His family is in the old world. Everything for which he has ever lived is in the old world, and he sets foot on the ship to sail into the unknown. To do this he must pull up his roots from the old world. On the other hand, the returning citizen has no such love for the country he has been visiting. His family is not there. His friends are not there. His business is not there. He does not really belong there. He can rejoice because he is setting foot on a vessel that will take him to the world to which he does belong. He is going home, he is going to people who know him and talk his language.

That is what makes the difference between the saint and the sinner, when it is time to die. Everyone of us must some-day board the ship of death. At such a time the sinner is fearful, and he weeps because he is forced to pull up roots in the only world with which he is familiar, and head out into the unknown. Whereas the saint sets foot on the ship of death with confidence and hope, and sometimes even rejoicing, because in a very real sense he is going home. He is headed for the land of which he is a citizen. The sinner shudders at death because he is interested in this world. The saint meets death with a steadfast hope because his interest is in the next world.

Destination

Finally, Paul makes it clear that there is a difference of destination. The terminal for the sinner is destruction: "whose end is destruction." The terminal for the saint is resurrection: "that it may be fashioned like unto His glorious body." The sinner lives his life with his allegiance to Satan, his objective to gratify the flesh, his sense of values to glory in his shame, his interest to mind earthly things, and his destination to be destroyed. The saint owes his allegiance to God, his objective is to crucify the flesh, his sense of values is to hate sin, his interest is in the next world, and his destination is resurrection.

In the seventh chapter of Matthew, Jesus says exactly the same thing: "Enter ye in at the strait gate: for wide is the gate, and broad is the way, that leadeth to destruction, and many there be which go in thereat; Because strait is the gate, and narrow is the way, which leadeth into life, and few there be that find it."

Conclusion

As Christians we must follow and model our lives after someone. We may choose to follow the sinner whom Paul has described in detail, or we may choose to follow the saint with whom Paul has associated himself. May God grant that we will make the right choice.

It is vitally important, not only because of its effect on us, but also because of its influence on others. We will follow someone, and someone will follow us.

Are you the kind of mother a daughter can follow? Would you want your son to go in his father's footsteps? Would you feel justified in saying to your Sunday School class, "Make me your example?"

The greatest missionary of all times was so certain of his relationship with the Lord, that he was able to write to the Christians of Philippi, "See that ye have us for an example."

The example of the missionary is not the *sinner* but the *saint*.

*   *   *

It is not maybe but must, not done but do, not systems but Satan, not civilization but Christ, not minor but major, not indefinite but immediate.

It is not men but money, not cash but credit, not charity but choice, not tithe but total, not privation but privilege.

It is not religion but regeneration, not goodness but God-liness, not complacency but concentration, not sinner but saint.

These are the mottoes that motivate the members, the money that moves the machinery, and the marks that make the missionary.